MORE
PARISH LITURGIES
EXPERIMENTS AND RESOURCES
IN SUNDAY WORSHIP

MORE PARISH LITURGIES

Experiments and Resources in Sunday Worship

by
Rev. Thomas Boyer

Editorial Assistant
Mary Sue Greer

PAULIST PRESS
New York / Paramus / Toronto

Library of Congress
Catalog Card Number: 73-81106

ISBN 0-8091-1777-0

Published by Paulist Press
Editorial Office: 1865 Broadway, N.Y., N.Y. 10023
Business Office: 400 Sette Drive, Paramus, N.J. 07652

Printed and bound in the
United States of America

CONTENTS

Contents

To Bishop Victor J. Reed

"Pastors of souls must therefore realize that, when the liturgy is celebrated, something more is required than the mere observation of the laws governing valid and licit celebration; it is their duty also to ensure that the faithful take part fully aware of what they are doing, actively engaged in the rite and enriched by its effects" (Article 11, *Constitution on the Sacred Liturgy*).

That "something more is required" Bishop Reed was beautifully aware of. He realized that we are not merely urged to see beyond the law and yield to people's needs, but that we are required to do so, balancing both demands on the scale of the Church's mission in this world.

The newness of life and attitudinal shifts which Vatican Council II tried to stir, Bishop Reed allowed to stir in himself. In the area of liturgy alone, Bishop Reed seemed to exemplify what the developments are about: flexibility. He knew there was a definite structure to liturgy, but one of its nature, variable—to suit a particular people, a particular occasion. His concern was not variety for its own sake, but rather as a deeper expression of the "catholic" nature of the Church. As once was the case, external uniformity was no longer the discipline needed to lead people in prayer. Bishop Reed saw liturgy less as ritual and words, but more as an action of God's people in prayer, and God being glorified because these assembled people were made more fully alive through a prayer-experience in having communion with their Father.

Bishop Reed's work on the Bishop's Committee on the Liturgy, his interest and support of the Southwest Liturgical Conference, his attitude toward variety and flexibility in our own diocese, can best be honored it seems, by our own hard work in providing a variety in the forms of prayer with the assemblies we lead. The liturgy is the expression and formation of what it really means to be, to become, to beget the people of God; this demands that we be really CATHOLIC: in touch with the diversity of needs and people who form the Church of God.

   With warmth and affection then, this book is dedicated to Victor J. Reed—a man who wore well and who blessed us by not being easily intimidated by other men or by ideas differing from his own.

THE ORDER OF CELEBRATION

I. The Entrance Rite

   A. Invitation to Worship
   B. Processional
   C. Greeting
      Penitential Rite
         (within penitential seasons: Advent and Lent)
   D. Prayer of Invocation

II. The Service of the Word

   A. First Reading
   B. Response
   C. Second Reading
   D. Response and/or Gospel Acclamation
   E. The Gospel
   F. Gospel Acclamation
   G. Homily
   H. Profession of Faith
   I. General Intentions
   J. Period of Reflection: Intermission
   K. Processional
   L. Prayer of Blessing over Gifts

III. The Table Prayer

   A. Preface
   B. Hymn of Praise
   C. Acclamation directly following Consecration
   D. Acclamation elaborating "Amen" at conclusion of
      Eucharistic Prayer

IV. The Service of Communion

   A. The "Our Father"
   B. Rite of Peace

About these books

The volumes you are holding are a diary. They are much like
the memories and experiences of a person recorded in privacy;
not out of fear of discovery, but rather out of the suspicion that
those things remembered and put away could be of interest to no
one. At the time it seemed that the only purpose for the writing
was to provide a measure with which to judge growth while
recognizing and recovering from error.

Thus we have the beginnings of PARISH LITURGIES. These
books should never be mistaken for some kind of recipe-books
for the production of "instant liturgy." A glance ahead should make
that very clear, for this is the diary of a community's life together;
a community that exists to pray and to serve. It is a community
that shares one thing with all others, the conviction that it is unique;
that there is not another like it.

A closer look reveals that it is a group of youthful people.
After all, the most avid diary keepers are usually the young. The
three priests who served this parish during the time of this diary
reflect the people themselves: two in their 20s and one in his 60s.
It was the same in the pews: many young people and a sizable
group of the old. If there is a generation gap, it was the missing
middle age who are out in the suburbs. Part of the mystery at the
Old Cathedral is that the young come, and the old stay with them.
Together they are the Word Made Flesh, the Body of Christ.

In that setting, anonymity is preserved for those of tender years
who are not yet able to risk identification. Yet there is also an
esprit de corps among those who have come long enough and
regularly enough to know one another by face and by name.
Between the two there is respect and the kind of understanding that
means support.

PREFACE

A glance at this second volume should make it obvious
that in the first year's growth, liturgy teams have found their
footing. The central place of the Gospel is now unequivocal to
those planning, and everything they prepare points to that
proclamation. The songs, the prayers, the other readings and
responses are all considered in light of how they may further
illumine the Gospel itself.

There is some indication in this volume that the "C cycle"
of readings was followed, but the arrangement for publication
does cause some of them to be out of order. The New Testament
reading before the Gospel has so often been problematic in terms
of theme development that in most cases it had to be changed
or omitted. It rarely proved relevant to the Gospel passage.

Nothing in these volumes substitutes for the most important
of all the parts of prayerful liturgy: the Homily. The best of these
liturgies is inadequate and empty without a Homily to bring it
all together. The Homily is the ultimate call to worship, the
invitation to conversion, that gives liturgy a chance to be what
we need it to be when we come together.

The bibliography of sources at the conclusion of each volume
should suggest still further references that will be of help in
planning liturgies. The list should grow daily. Along with our list
of books, newspapers, and magazines have accumulated the names
and lives of people who have contributed to this second volume.
To the names of those noted in the previous volume must be
added the community of the Sisters of Mercy at Mt. St. Mary's;
some of these Eucharistic celebrations come from their chapel
with little revision for parochial use. Along with the sisters we
must acknowledge Father Tom McSherry who has proven (although
I am certain it has not been easy) that these beginnings were no
fad or personality cult. For even though some of the pastors have
changed, the tradition of prayer and worship that these volumes
witness continues. It is an affirmation of his own personal

convictions and holiness that this tradition continues. To all those presently contributing to the quality of the worship experience with him, we are grateful for the hope they give. May they continue to proclaim: "Christ has died, Christ is risen, Christ will come again."

FIRST SUNDAY OF ADVENT II

Theme: Waiting for Something

THE ENTRANCE RITE

INVITATION TO WORSHIP:

On this, the first Sunday of Advent, we find ourselves waiting
and praying for the coming of a Savior who will be the
fullfillment of all our desires. Advent is a season set aside to
nourish hope and trust.

Let us think of Advent as a period of "Waiting for
Some-THING":

Waiting for the seasons to change and watching in awe as
the land and its produce show forth change.

Waiting for the sunrise to help us begin our day.

Waiting for the day of your marriage during the days of
your engagement.

Waiting for the sound of your baby's cry expressing its
need of you—or the call of your children's voices as they
rush in from school.

Waiting for a telephone call, a visit, a letter when you are
alone—or far away from family and friends.

Waiting for the unknown—for the unspecified thing—a
some-thing of importance.

Waiting now for Father to greet us with his blessing and
to pray for us in the name of the Lord Jesus Christ.

PROCESSIONAL:

"The Coming of Our God," *People's Mass Book,* #6.

GREETING:

Eucharistic Liturgies, p. 143.

PENITENTIAL RITE:

(*Response:* Lord, have mercy.)

That by your Word we may see our sinful desire to avoid
the needs of those who live in our city, especially the
young and the old, we pray to you, O Lord:

1

That by your Word we may see that we sin by attempting
to apply our answers to everyman's struggle to become
himself, we pray to you, O Lord:

That by your Word we may see our sin in failing to accept
ourselves as you have made us, weak, wanting, but yet a
people who have reason to hope, we pray to you, O Lord:

PRAYER OF INVOCATION:
Eucharistic Liturgies, p. 143.

THE SERVICE OF THE WORD

FIRST READING:
Isaiah 63:16b–17; 64:1–7(8).
(Celebrant lights Paschal Candle during following response.)

RESPONSE:
Ps. 80:1a–2, 8–9, 14b–15, 17 *(by reader)*. Ps. 80:19 *(by people
—alternated with verses above)*.

SECOND READING:
1 Corinthians 1:3–9.

GOSPEL ACCLAMATION:
"Send Forth Your Light and Your Truth" (Ps. 42, Antiphon
II), *Twenty-Four Psalms and a Canticle,* p. 20.
*(During this antiphon, the celebrant carries the Paschal Candle
to the Advent Wreath and uses it to light the first candle.)*

THE GOSPEL:
Mark 13:33–37.

GOSPEL ACCLAMATION:
Repeat from above.

HOMILY

GENERAL INTENTIONS:
(Response: Lord, hear our prayer.)
That during Advent our waiting be more than a sentimental

preparation; that we never lose sight of the primary
meaning, we pray to the Lord:

That we not end this celebration today but go out of here
sharing our faith, our hope, and our trust with those who
live among us, let us pray to the Lord:

That our waiting be nourished with a holy impatience as we
say, "Come, Lord Jesus, Come quickly!" we pray to the
Lord:

PERIOD OF REFLECTION:
Intermission

PROCESSIONAL:
"O God, Our Help in Ages Past," *People's Mass Book*, #185.

PRAYER OF BLESSING OVER GIFTS:
Eucharistic Liturgies, p. 144.

THE TABLE PRAYER

PREFACE:
"Advent I," *The English-Latin Sacramentary*.

HYMN OF PRAISE:
"Praise to the Lord," first verse, *People's Mass Book*, #175.

ACCLAMATION AT CONSECRATION:
#235a, *People's Mass Book*.

ENDING ACCLAMATION:
"Praise to the Lord," third verse, *People's Mass Book*, #175.

THE SERVICE OF COMMUNION

THE "OUR FATHER"

RITE OF PEACE

FRACTION RITE:
Litany of the "Lamb of God"

SONG:
"O Come, O Come, Emmanuel," *People's Mass Book,* #1.

PERIOD OF REFLECTION:
Intermission

THE DISMISSAL RITE

PRAYER OF BENEDICTION:
Eucharistic Liturgies, p. 144.

BLESSING AND DISMISSAL

ANNOUNCEMENTS

RECESSIONAL:
"Maranatha," *People's Mass Book,* #8.

SECOND SUNDAY OF ADVENT II

Theme: Waiting for Somebody

THE ENTRANCE RITE

INVITATION TO WORSHIP:
"Waiting for Somebody," *Sign*, Dec. 1969, p. 21.

PROCESSIONAL:
"The Coming of Our God," *People's Mass Book*, #6.

GREETING:
Eucharistic Liturgies, p. 145.

PENITENTIAL RITE:
(*Response:* Lord, have mercy.)
That by your Word we may see our sinfulness in failing
to accept your words as a source of man's peace and,
instead, substituting our own words, let us pray to the Lord:
That by your Word we may see our sin of adding despair
to the world because of our unwillingness to trust and to
hope in one another, let us pray to the Lord:
That by your Word we may see that the lack of Christ's
presence among men today is partially a result of our
failure to live by the words he has spoken to us, let us
pray to the Lord:

PRAYER OF INVOCATION:
Eucharistic Liturgies, p. 145.

THE SERVICE OF THE WORD

FIRST READING:
H. J. Mueller in *Horizons of Hope*, p. 83.

RESPONSE:
Introduction, p. 59, *Horizons of Hope*.

5

SECOND READING:
Philippians 1:3–6, 8–11.

GOSPEL ACCLAMATION:
"Send Forth Your Light and Your Truth" (Ps. 42, Antiphon
II), *Twenty-Four Psalms and a Canticle*, p. 20.
*(While this antiphon is being sung, the celebrant lights
two candles on the Advent Wreath.)*

THE GOSPEL:
Matthew 11:2–11.

GOSPEL ACCLAMATION:
Repeat from above.

HOMILY

GENERAL INTENTIONS:
(*Response:* Lord, hear our prayer.)
For those still standing in darkness who have not yet seen
the light of hope, we pray to the Lord:
For the poor and oppressed who are still awaiting the justice
and freedom brought to us by Christ, we pray to the Lord:
For all who are traveling during this season that they will
remain safe, we pray to the Lord:
For all those who have yet to find the cause for hope and
joy, we pray to the Lord:

PERIOD OF REFLECTION:
Intermission

PROCESSIONAL:
"Maranatha," *People's Mass Book*, #8.

PRAYER OF BLESSING OVER GIFTS:
Eucharistic Liturgies, p. 146.

THE TABLE PRAYER

PREFACE:
"Advent I," *The English-Latin Sacramentary.*

HYMN OF PRAISE:
"Praise to the Lord," first verse, *People's Mass Book,* #175.

ACCLAMATION AT CONSECRATION:
#235a, *People's Mass Book.*

ENDING ACCLAMATION:
"Praise to the Lord," third verse, *People's Mass Book,* #175.

THE SERVICE OF COMMUNION

THE "OUR FATHER"

RITE OF PEACE

FRACTION RITE:
Litany of the "Lamb of God"

SONG:
"Peace My Friends," *Hymnal for Young Christians,* Vol. II,
p. 34.

PERIOD OF REFLECTION:
Intermission

THE DISMISSAL RITE

PRAYER OF BENEDICTION:
Eucharistic Liturgies, p. 146.

BLESSING AND DISMISSAL

ANNOUNCEMENTS

RECESSIONAL:
"O Come, O Come, Emmanuel," *People's Mass Book,* #1.

THIRD SUNDAY OF ADVENT II

Theme: Waiting with Somebody

THE ENTRANCE RITE

INVITATION TO WORSHIP:

At this mid-point in Advent we today reflect upon our anticipation of the Christmas festival in terms of "Waiting with Somebody." That is to say, we remind ourselves that we are all, together, as a people, involved in the mystery of the Word becoming flesh; for it was to a people that Christ was born, a people who had for generations sensed their incompleteness. They waited together, comforting one another, caring for each other in anxious moments of birth and death. As the Christmas cards and greetings begin flowing again this year in the attempt to bridge the miles between friends and family members, we become aware of our need for one another. Let us now pull ourselves together as a worshiping community in praise and thanksgiving to the Father who has spoken to us in his Son, Jesus, who is still taking flesh in us.

PROCESSIONAL:

"As We Await the Lord," *Biblical Hymns and Psalms,* p. 12.

GREETING:

May the Lord bless us and fill us with his peace
as together, we the Church, try to bring
God's Word to a waiting, anxious world.

PENITENTIAL RITE:

(*Response:* Lord, have mercy.)

That by your Word and your holy Incarnation we may
realize that whatsoever we do to the least of our brothers
is done also to you, we pray to the Lord:

That by your Word we may be more sensitive to your
becoming flesh through our lives, we pray to the Lord:

8

That by your Word made flesh in our faith, the face of the earth might be renewed, we pray to the Lord:

PRAYER OF INVOCATION:
Collect, First Sunday of Advent, *The English-Latin Sacramentary.*

THE SERVICE OF THE WORD

FIRST READING:
"Waiting with Somebody," *Sign*, Dec. 1969, p. 22.

RESPONSE:
Silent reflection.

SECOND READING:
Philippians 4:4–9.

GOSPEL ACCLAMATION:
"Maranatha," *People's Mass Book*, #8.
(Three candles of Advent Wreath are lighted.)

THE GOSPEL:
Luke 3:10–18.

GOSPEL ACCLAMATION:
Repeat from above.

HOMILY

GENERAL INTENTIONS:
(*Response:* Lord, hear our prayer.)
That, in waiting for the reunion of our families at Christmas, we will remember the presence of Christ among us, we pray to the Lord:
That, in anticipation of the real spirit of Christmas, we will concentrate more on the spirit of giving than of receiving, we pray to the Lord:
That we strive to accept all the hustle and bustle of preparing

for the anniversary of Jesus' coming with the spirit of love and giving that the Holy Family manifested, we pray to the Lord:

PERIOD OF REFLECTION:
Intermission

PROCESSIONAL:
"Joy to the World," *People's Mass Book*, #13.

PRAYER OF BLESSING OVER GIFTS:
Eucharistic Liturgies, p. 148.

THE TABLE PRAYER

PREFACE:
"Eucharistic Prayer of Human Unity," *The Experimental Liturgy Book*, p. 100.

HYMN OF PRAISE:
"Sing Praise to Our Creator," *People's Mass Book*, #43.

ACCLAMATION AT CONSECRATION:
#235a, *People's Mass Book*.

ENDING ACCLAMATION:
"You Alone Are Holy," *Biblical Hymns and Psalms*, Vol. II, p. 52.

THE SERVICE OF COMMUNION

THE "OUR FATHER"

RITE OF PEACE

FRACTION RITE:
Litany of the "Lamb of God"

SONG:
"The King of Glory," *People's Mass Book*, #7.

PERIOD OF REFLECTION:
   Intermission

THE DISMISSAL RITE

PRAYER OF BENEDICTION:
   Eucharistic Liturgies, p. 148.

BLESSING AND DISMISSAL

ANNOUNCEMENTS

RECESSIONAL:
   "Come, O Lord! O Come for Our Saving," *Biblical Hymns
   and Psalms,* p. 14.

FOURTH SUNDAY OF ADVENT II

Theme: Expectation
*(This liturgy emphasizes the value of silence. The celebrant
enters in silence and immediately begins the Penitential Rite.)*

PENITENTIAL RITE:
(Response: Forgive us our failures, O Lord.*)*

Celebrant: As we await the Lord let us call to mind those
attitudes which we may have which would blind and deafen
us when he does come among us: *(pause)* Lord Jesus, you
have said: "How happy are the poor in spirit; theirs is the
kingdom of heaven."

Parishioner: For depending excessively upon material goods as
the source of man's joy and security rather than upon the
simple and honest truth of Christ's Word, we pray to you,
O Lord:

Celebrant: Lord Jesus, you have said: "Happy the gentle: they
shall have the earth for their heritage."

Parishioner: For failing to be tolerant of those whose opinions
differ from our own and for failing to recognize the sincerity
of another's ideas, we pray to you, O Lord:

Celebrant: Lord Jesus, you have said: "Happy those who mourn:
they shall be comforted."

Parishioner: For failing to spend time *and* ourselves with the
lonely who are: the young, the elderly, the alcoholic, the
addict, the neurotic, the sick, the sorrowful—any and all of
whom we may find among our own family and friends, we
pray to you, O Lord:

Celebrant: Lord Jesus, you have said: "Happy those who hunger
and thirst for what is right: they shall be satisfied."

Parishioner: For the times when, because of the immensity of
the problems of the world, nation and state, we have hidden
from *(name of city)* problems of inadequate education for
many, proper housing for those dispossessed by urban renewal,
and insufficient wages that hold people in poverty, we pray
to you, O Lord:

Celebrant: Lord Jesus, you have said: "Happy the merciful: they shall have mercy shown them."

Parishioner: For failing to extend forgiveness in those situations in which we ourselves have asked forgiveness: we pray to you, O Lord:

Celebrant: Lord Jesus, you have said: "Happy the pure in heart: they shall see God."

Parishioner: For our failure to be honest and sincere with ourselves and thus often excluding ourselves from the Christian community, we pray to you, O Lord:

Celebrant: Lord Jesus, you have said: "Happy the peacemakers: they shall be called sons of God."

Parishioner: For failing to say: "I love you," "I'll try to understand," "Let's work it out together," "I forgive you," and other such words—for failing to make these sounds of love which can bring peace: we pray to you, O Lord:

Celebrant: Lord Jesus, you have said: "Happy those who are persecuted in the cause of right; theirs is the kingdom of heaven."

Parishioner: For the times that we choose to discredit the Christian behavior of others so as to justify our own actions: we pray to you, O Lord:

PRAYER OF INVOCATION:

"Lord God, we see the sins of the world," *Your Word Is Near*, p. 131. Add this or similar ending: "We ask this in Jesus' name who with you and the Spirit lives as God forever and ever."

THE SERVICE OF THE WORD

FIRST READING:
Isaiah 40:3–5.

RESPONSE:
Silent reflection on these questions, which should be printed on the program for this liturgy:
Is the wilderness of Isaiah a matter of history or do we not

find ourselves wandering, searching in the wilderness even
today?
Have we not left unfilled valleys of distrust and suspicion
and have we not raised up mountains of arrogance and
self-righteousness in relation to our fellow man?
Do we understand that until we make a turnabout, convert,
and allow the power of God's Word to dictate to us, the glory
of God cannot be revealed so that all mankind may see it?

SECOND READING:
Zephaniah 3:9–14.

RESPONSE:
Isaiah 11:1–9.
(Four candles of Advent Wreath are lighted).

THE GOSPEL:
John 3:29–30. Preface with "John the Baptist said:"

HOMILY:
The celebrant could paraphrase the section of Martin Luther
King's sermon, "I Have A Dream," *My Life with Martin
Luther King, Jr.,* pp. 239–240, and then allow for meditation;
or simply follow Gospel with a meditation period. If this
liturgy is being used as a penance service, confessions could
be heard at this time.

PERIOD OF REFLECTION:
Intermission

THE TABLE PRAYER

PREFACE:
We thank you, Almighty Father, for the sake
    of your Son, Jesus Christ, the Word made flesh.
The prophets longed to see his coming,
    and we have seen it.
Israel groaned to see the dawning of a new creation
    in the one whom you would send;

and we have not only witnessed this dawn,
but have seen the light of the world
rise to a brightness beyond imagination.
In thanksgiving we praise you
for sending us your Son,
yet in joyful hope we await his coming in glory;
we await your mercy to open our eyes and ears
to his presence now
so that we might be filled with his Spirit
and become more brilliant witnesses
of the light which he is.
With all of creation, anxious for a new world of
light and love,
we blend our voices, saying:

HYMN OF PRAISE:
(*Spoken*) From *The English-Latin Sacramentary.*

ACCLAMATION AT CONSECRATION:
(*Spoken*) Lyrics from "Keep In Mind," *People's Mass Book,*
#145.

THE SERVICE OF COMMUNION

THE "OUR FATHER"

RITE OF PEACE

FRACTION RITE:
Litany of the "Lamb of God"

PERIOD OF REFLECTION:
Intermission

THE DISMISSAL RITE

PRAYER OF BENEDICTION:
"You do not deny or make light of our sins," *Your Word Is
Near,* p. 135.

BLESSING AND DISMISSAL

ANNOUNCEMENTS

RECESSIONAL:
   (Ministers walk out in silence.)

THE FEAST OF CHRISTMAS II
(Including the Solemn Closing of Advent)

Theme: "Today and Here and In Those Days"
The greater part of this liturgy is taken from the script given
by Huub Oosterhuis in *Prayers, Poems & Songs,* pp. 73–95
for a Christmas Eve liturgical celebration. Exceptions are
noted.

THE SERVICE OF THE WORD
The Solemn Closing of Advent

PROCESSION OF LIGHT:
The lights in the church are extinguished; minister(s) enter
bearing the lighted Paschal Candle, which is finally placed
beside the crib. All are singing, "Come, O Lord! O Come
for Our Saving" (Is. 9:1–6, Antiphon II), *Biblical Hymns and
Psalms,* p. 14.

FIRST READING:
The "Opening Song" on p. 76 of Oosterhuis' script. *(The first
three readings are read by the light of the Paschal Candle.)*

RESPONSE:
"As We Await the Lord," *Biblical Hymns and Psalms,* p. 12.

SECOND READING:
Reading 1, p. 77 of Oosterhuis' script.

RESPONSE:
"O Come, O Come, Emmanuel," *People's Mass Book,* #1. *(All
candles are lighted.)*

THIRD READING:
Reading 2, p. 78 of Oosterhuis' script.

RESPONSE:
"O Little Town of Bethlehem" (from any standard hymnal).

(All lights are turned on. Remainder of readings are done from pulpit.)

FOURTH READING:
Reading 3, p. 79 of Oosterhuis' script.

RESPONSE:
"Silent Night," Joseph Mohr, *People's Mass Book,* #12.

FIFTH READING:
Reading 4, p. 80 of Oosterhuis' script.

RESPONSE:
"Hark! the Herald Angels Sing," *People's Mass Book,* #10.

READING OF THE MARTYROLOGY:
"The Liturgical Announcement of the Birth of Christ," edited and prepared by Joseph T. Kush, C.G.M.

RESPONSE:
"The First Noel," *People's Mass Book,* #11.

THE GOSPEL:
Translation on p. 81 of Oosterhuis' script.

RESPONSE:
"Angels We Have Heard on High," *People's Mass Book,* #16. This spoken response follows immediately: "Verses from Psalm 18," p. 80 of Oosterhuis' script.

HOMILY

PROFESSION OF FAITH:
The Apostles' Creed.

GENERAL INTENTIONS:
(*Response:* Prince of Peace, hear our prayer.)
Pages 93–94 of Oosterhuis' script followed by prayer on p. 95.

PERIOD OF REFLECTION:
Intermission

PROCESSIONAL:
"O Come, All Ye Faithful," *People's Mass Book,* #9.

PRAYER OF BLESSING OVER GIFTS:
Eucharistic Liturgies, p. 152.

THE TABLE PRAYER

PREFACE:
First stanza of "The Table Prayer," p. 88 of Oosterhuis' script.
Add "Therefore we join with all creation in one great hymn
of praise":

HYMN OF PRAISE:
"Holy, Holy, Holy! Lord God Almighty." *People's Mass Book,*
#184.

ACCLAMATION AT CONSECRATION:
#235a, *People's Mass Book.*

ENDING ACCLAMATION
#108b, *People's Mass Book.*

THE SERVICE OF COMMUNION

THE "OUR FATHER"

RITE OF PEACE

FRACTION RITE:
Litany of the "Lamb of God"

SONG:
"Unto Us A Child Is Born" (Is. 9:1–6, Antiphon I), *Biblical
Hymns and Psalms,* p. 14.

PERIOD OF REFLECTION:
    Intermission

THE DISMISSAL RITE

PRAYER OF BENEDICTION:
    Eucharistic Liturgies, p. 152.

BLESSING AND DISMISSAL

ANNOUNCEMENTS

RECESSIONAL:
    "Joy to the World," *People's Mass Book,* #13.

SUNDAY WITHIN THE OCTAVE OF CHRISTMAS II

Theme: Christmas Joy Is: The Power to Dream

THE ENTRANCE RITE

INVITATION TO WORSHIP:
> *Sign,* Dec. 1970, p. 6, beginning with "Dreamers are the
> makers of human culture," ending with "And he gives his
> brothers the power to dream with him."

PROCESSIONAL:
> "O Come, All Ye Faithful," *People's Mass Book,* #9.

GREETING:
> Peace and joy to you who live by the knowledge
>   that God our Father has manifested
>   his love for us
>   by sending us his Son, our Lord Jesus.

PRAYER OF INVOCATION:
> Mindful of our Father's goodness toward us,
>   let us pray:
> Father, your Son has burst forth in our world, a new light
>   to scatter the darkness of our minds.
> By choosing that he come to maturity
>   within the family,
>   you have revealed to us
>   the dignity of the human family.
> We ask that you bless all those
>   who are assembled here.
> As members of families, make us realize
>   the sources of growth and richness
>   which each individual can offer to the family
>   and to the entire human community.
> We ask this in the name of Jesus,
>   who with you and the Holy Spirit,
>   lives as God, forever and ever.
> (First sentence from *Eucharistic Liturgies,* p. 154)

THE SERVICE OF THE WORD

FIRST READING:
Rudolf Bultmann in *Horizons of Hope,* p. 89.

RESPONSE:
Isaiah 11:6–9.

SECOND READING:
Colossians 3:12–21.

GOSPEL ACCLAMATION:
"Alleluia, Alleluia, Alleluia," (Ps. 150), *People's Mass Book,*
#163.

THE GOSPEL:
Luke 2:41–52.

RESPONSE:
Verse from "O Little Town of Bethlehem" (*from any standard hymnal*):
"O holy Child of Bethlehem!
"Descend to us, we pray . . ."

HOMILY

GENERAL INTENTIONS:
(*Response:* O Lord, hear our prayer.)
For patience to listen and openness to understand—that such
    qualities be found in all Christians, especially those who
    live as families, we pray to the Lord:
That young people might realize and appreciate all that
    previous generations have accomplished by their vision and
    sincere labors, we pray to the Lord:
For older generations that they might be thankful for and
    considerate of the dreams of the younger people and
    encourage the sincere hopes of the young, we pray to the
    Lord:
That the family of man might more actively cooperate in

those actions which can benefit all of us who are brothers
both by reason of our common desires and our common
hope in the Gospel message of the Lord, we pray to the
Lord:

That the service of love which Christ encouraged among all
men might be our source of hope as a people who seek to
live as one family, we pray to the Lord:

PERIOD OF REFLECTION:
Intermission

PROCESSIONAL:
"Hark! The Herald Angels Sing," *People's Mass Book,* #10.

PRAYER OF BLESSING OVER GIFTS:
Father, in your wisdom and goodness, you have chosen
that men should come to a fullness of life
and learn to dream
within the context of the family.
Take this bread and this wine as signs from our hands
that we are eager to serve you
in the role which you have given us,
and anxious to make real the dream you have for men.
All glory be to you, Father, and to your Son,
through whom we ask you for all that we need,
and through whom you give us all that is good.
We sing praise to your name, now and forever.
(Adapted from *Eucharistic Liturgies,* p. 155.)

THE TABLE PRAYER

PREFACE:
First stanza of "The Table Prayer," *Prayers, Poems & Songs,*
p. 88. Add "Therefore we join with all creation in singing
your praise:"

HYMN OF PRAISE:
"Angels We Have Heard on High," *People's Mass Book,* #16.

ACCLAMATION AT CONSECRATION:
#235a, *People's Mass Book.*

ENDING ACCLAMATION:
#108b, *People's Mass Book.*

THE SERVICE OF COMMUNION

THE "OUR FATHER"

RITE OF PEACE

FRACTION RITE:
Litany of the "Lamb of God"

SONG:
"Unto Us A Child Is Born" (Is. 9:1–6, Antiphon I), *Biblical Hymns and Psalms*, p. 14.

PERIOD OF REFLECTION:
Intermission

THE DISMISSAL RITE

PRAYER OF BENEDICTION:
Father, we thank you for the ability to dream,
 the strength to fulfill our dreams.
May we always rejoice in all men—
 the young who dream dreams
 and the old who see visions.
Grant that in all families
 and in the one family of man
 there may grow among us the wisdom and charity
 to see the value of all those
 who seek for growth and understanding.
May we always respect the sincerity
 of those dreamers among us.
We ask this in Jesus' name

who with you and the Spirit
lives as God, forever and ever.

BLESSING AND DISMISSAL

ANNOUNCEMENTS

RECESSIONAL:
"Joy to the World," *People's Mass Book,* #13.

THE FESTIVAL OF MARY THE MOTHER OF GOD II
January 1

Theme: God Sent His Son, Born of a Woman

THE ENTRANCE RITE

INVITATION TO WORSHIP:

Today's feast points to the mother of Jesus as a sign to us
of the totality of Christ's humanness. As St. Paul explains in
the second reading, the birth of Jesus from Mary is part
and parcel of the human condition he adopted. On Christmas
Day we were impressed with the divine condition of the
Christ-child by the events which surrounded the
announcement of his birth to the shepherds. Today, on the
Octave Day of Christmas, we remind ourselves of the human
condition of the Christ-child by remembering that he was
born of woman, of Mary, who has become the Mother of
God's people, his chosen race, his Church.

PROCESSIONAL:

"O Come, All Ye Faithful," *People's Mass Book*, #9.

GREETING:

Welcome to you who have chosen to begin
   this first day of the new year
   in praise and thanksgiving to God our Father.
May the peace of this Christmas season
   gain a new hold on your hearts,
   and may the spirit of Christ-born-among-men
   be with you.

PRAYER OF INVOCATION:

Mindful that today we may begin again to make ourselves
   new-people with this new year, we pray:
All things are recreated and made new
   through your Son Jesus, Eternal Father;
   and so on this day of new beginnings—
   this first day of New Year,

we seek to be made new in our human condition
by remembering what you have done
to the human by the incarnation.
The first to be made-new was the Virgin Mary.
We praise you and bless your holy name
for what you have done in her.
With her as model, we cannot fail
to be part of the Word-made-flesh
and part of your life.
All honor and glory be to you, Father,
through your Son, Jesus Christ,
who with the Spirit lives as God
forever and ever.

THE SERVICE OF THE WORD

FIRST READING:

Numbers 6:22–27. Introduction: The first reading is a selection from the book of Numbers where, in one word, we find the priestly blessing made over the people after the morning sacrifice. The priest prayed for the preservation of the people, then for the prosperity for all under God's gaze and favor; finally God's complete blessing is invoked—peace: the sum total of all they could desire. This peace enters the world at Jesus' birth.

RESPONSE:

Ps. 67:1–2, 4, 5, 6a–7 (*by reader*). "May God bless us in his mercy" (*alternated by people with verses from psalm given above*).

SECOND READING:

Galatians 4:4–7. Introduction: The second reading today is from Paul's letter to the Galatians. This passage contains the core of Paul's teaching in that the mission of God's Son was to make us grow up, to free us from a minority spent in subjection to the Old Testament law, and to make us through his Spirit full sons of God's household. Paradoxically, Christ did this by subjecting himself to the law of his people, Israel.

GOSPEL ACCLAMATION:
   "Sion, Sing," *People's Mass Book*, #165.

THE GOSPEL:
   Luke 2:16–21.

RESPONSE:
   "The First Noel," *People's Mass Book*, #11.

HOMILY

PROFESSION OF FAITH

PERIOD OF REFLECTION:
   Intermission

PROCESSIONAL:
   "Unto Us A Child Is Born" (Is. 9, 1–6, Antiphon I), *Biblical Hymns and Psalms*, p. 14.

PRAYER OF BLESSING OVER GIFTS:
   Father, we come before you with gladness and joy,
      setting before you bread and wine
      to speak of our joy, to say
      that we are pleased to be your people,
      and grateful for the life your Son promises us.
   Hear our prayers and welcome us in your sight,
      and by your most holy power transform us
      that we may make real upon the earth
      the message of peace
      which you speak to us today.
   All glory be to you,
      and to your Son, now and forever and ever.

THE TABLE PRAYER

PREFACE:
   We thank you, all powerful and loving Father of all men,
      for sharing with us the love that makes you one

with your Son and with the Spirit,
for your life is one only of love.
We praise you and thank you
for calling us through faith
to share your gift of love
with the world which you care for
to the extent of sending your Son to be one of us.
You have called us not to be idle,
or live for ourselves,
but to raise up cities from the ground
and sing new songs in the air,
and hasten the fulfillment of your promise
to reunite the world and all men in your Son,
Jesus Christ our Lord.
With loving gratitude, we bless your name;
and lifting our voices in the chorus of creation,
we celebrate your constant presence
with this hymn of praise:
(Adapted from "Eucharistic Prayer of Human Unity" and
"The Canon of the Pilgrim Church," *The Experimental
Liturgy Book*, pp. 84 and 73, respectively.)

HYMN OF PRAISE:
"Angels We Have Heard On High," *People's Mass Book*, #16.

ACCLAMATION AT CONSECRATION:
"Keep in Mind," *People's Mass Book*, #145.

ENDING ACCLAMATION:
#108b, *People's Mass Book*.

THE SERVICE OF COMMUNION

THE "OUR FATHER"

RITE OF PEACE

FRACTION RITE:
Litany of the "Lamb of God"

SONG:
 "The Church's One Foundation," *People's Mass Book*, #223.

PERIOD OF REFLECTION:
 Intermission

THE DISMISSAL RITE

PRAYER OF BENEDICTION:
 All glory and praise be to you, Father,
  who have drawn us from all across this city.
 We praise the deeds
  you have accomplished among men.
 On this day of new beginnings,
  we pledge ourselves again
  to be faithful to your Word,
  to fulfill and complete the role
  begun by Mary the Mother of your Son—
  which is the giving flesh to your Word;
  a Word which is love,
  which is forgiveness,
  which is peace.
 We seek to do these things
  through your Son Jesus,
  who is now living with you and your Spirit
  forever and ever.

BLESSING AND DISMISSAL

ANNOUNCEMENTS

RECESSIONAL:
 "Rejoice the Lord Is King," *Hymnal for Young Christians*,
 p. 115.

EPIPHANY SUNDAY II

Theme: "Your Light Has Come"

THE ENTRANCE RITE

INVITATION TO WORSHIP:
Alastair Reid, *To Be Alive!*, beginning with "We bring the sun . . ." and ending with "Take my hand."

PROCESSIONAL:
"The First Noel," *People's Mass Book*, #11.

GREETING:
To you who have come seeking light and life
from God's Word-made-flesh,
I give peace.
For like the earth before the creation of light,
our life without Christ is barren and unproductive;
but by the incarnation light has come into the world;
that light is Christ Jesus the Lord.

PRAYER OF INVOCATION:
Grateful for the light of Christ which touches our lives in so
many ways, let us pray:
Father, we your people now rise up in splendor
to sing and acknowledge your greatness.
For by the holy incarnation of your Son,
a light has come into human life which,
as the rising sun warms and brings the quiet cold
earth to life,
has stirred new life within us.
By this light, Jesus,
your glory shines in us for all men to see.
We give you all praise and thanksgiving
through Jesus your Son who with the Spirit
lives and reigns forever and ever.
(Introduction from *Eucharistic Liturgies*, p. 160.)

THE SERVICE OF THE WORD

FIRST READING:
Isaiah 60: 1–6.

RESPONSE:
"Creation," *Life*, Jan. 12, 1971, all of page 18. Response is followed by a short period of silent reflection.

THE GOSPEL:
John 1:1–12a, 14.

RESPONSE:
Number 5, *Prayers, Poems & Songs*, p. 31.

HOMILY

GENERAL INTENTIONS:
(*Response:* Lord, hear our prayer.)
For those who suffer from the cold because of inadequate housing and clothing, let us pray to the Lord:
For those who are troubled over decisions, that their choices will be illuminated by the Good News of Christ living among men, and that the new fellowship which this news brings will give all men a new sense of responsibility for their brother, let us pray to the Lord:
For those who are saddened and discouraged by their difficulties in life, that they might find strength in our sharing of their burdens, let us pray to the Lord:
For those who are facing death, that their faith may give them courage, that our love might give them hope, let us pray to the Lord:
For our young people, that they may seek and find understanding and support as they search to find their way in life, let us pray to the Lord:

PERIOD OF REFLECTION:
Intermission

PROCESSIONAL:
"Thou Whose Almighty Word," *The Hymnal of the
Protestant Episcopal Church in the United States of America,*
#272.

PRAYER OF BLESSING OVER GIFTS:
Father, we have gathered together
 from all parts of this city
 to set before you this sign of our faith.
As your Word has taken flesh through Jesus your Son,
 so now we seek to unite ourselves in this same mystery,
 that by these signs of mutual giving
 we ourselves might have life in all its fullness.
All glory be to you through your Son Jesus
 through whom we make this prayer,
 now and forever and ever.

THE TABLE PRAYER

PREFACE:
"Canon of the Light of God," *The Experimental Liturgy
Book,* p. 82.

HYMN OF PRAISE:
"Praise God, From Whom All Blessings Flow," *People's Mass
Book,* #45.

ACCLAMATION AT CONSECRATION:
#190b, *People's Mass Book.*

ENDING ACCLAMATION:
#108b, *People's Mass Book.*

THE SERVICE OF COMMUNION

THE "OUR FATHER"

RITE OF PEACE

FRACTION RITE:
   Litany of the "Lamb of God"

SONG:
   "Send Forth Your Light and Your Truth" (Ps. 42, Antiphon
   II), *Twenty-Four Psalms and a Canticle*, p. 20.

MEDITATION READING:
   Matthew 2:1–12.

RESPONSE:
   Same quote as in Invitation to Worship in this liturgy.

THE DISMISSAL RITE

PRAYER OF BENEDICTION:
   Everlasting Father, your glory is made known to men
       through your Son Jesus Christ.
   We who have now become members of his body
       through this sacrament
       are now the signs of your peace in our world.
   May we who have received your gift of love
       proclaim that love to all men.
   We ask this through Jesus your Son
       who lives and reigns forever and ever.
   (Adapted from *Eucharistic Liturgies*, p. 161.)

BLESSING AND DISMISSAL

ANNOUNCEMENTS

RECESSIONAL:
   Same as Processional, third verse.

FIRST SUNDAY AFTER EPIPHANY II

Theme: Man's Search for His Life's Purpose

THE ENTRANCE RITE

INVITATION TO WORSHIP:

The life of a man is a continuous reaching out, a constant
moving toward the next goal. Yet, even as he stretches and
groans and, in attaining his prize, rejoices, there is a gnawing
question inside himself—why? Why do I run on eagerly? What
is the purpose of my life? Am I doing the right thing,
making the right decision? And the questions leave him
unsettled, unsure. We come together today as Christians to
reflect on these questions. While no answers may come to us,
perhaps we can find some direction, some encouragement
from our God, who speaks to us through his Word; who
comes to us in the man next to us.

PROCESSIONAL:

"Thou Whose Almighty Word," *The Hymnal of the Protestant
Episcopal Church in the United States of America,* #272.

GREETING:

May the Lord our God in all his goodness bless you.
May he share with you his loving kindness.
May you be filled with peace.

PRAYER OF INVOCATION:

God our Father, as we look at our lives
  and the world which swirls about us,
    it is not easy to remain calm and unafraid.
In our weakness we look
  to the Word of your Son for some hint
  as to the reason for our existence.
Open us, our Father, to your presence here
  this day so that we may truly
  see you and hear you.

35

We ask this in the name of Jesus, your Son,
who with you and the Spirit,
lives as God forever and ever.

THE SERVICE OF THE WORD

FIRST READING:
James Branch Cabell in *Horizons of Hope,* p. 139.

RESPONSE:
Robert O. Johann in *Horizons of Hope,* p. 139.

SECOND READING:
1 Corinthians 2:7–10.

GOSPEL ACCLAMATION:
"Alleluia, Alleluia, Alleluia" (Ps. 150), *People's Mass Book,*
#163; followed by "Psalm 8," *Prayers, Poems & Songs,* p. 120.

THE GOSPEL:
Matthew 3:13–17.

GOSPEL ACCLAMATION:
Repeat "Alleluia" from above.

HOMILY

GENERAL INTENTIONS:
(*Response:* Lord, hear our prayer.)
For the growers of citrus fruits in this country and throughout
the world, whose crops have been damaged or destroyed
by the cold, that they not lose hope but have the courage
to begin again, we pray to you, O Lord:
For those who find the days of winter to be a time of loneliness
and inactivity; that those of us who call ourselves lovers of
men might enliven their days by means of time spent with
them, we pray to you, O Lord:
For those working with the mentally retarded, the incurably
ill, the insane, the criminal and the delinquent, that they

persevere in their efforts and perhaps receive some small
reward of success, we pray to you, O Lord:
For ourselves, that as the succeeding days with all their
responsibilities, their triumphs and failures, crowd upon
us, we have vision enough to see the purpose of our days
and the meaning of our own personal life, we pray to
you, O Lord:

PERIOD OF REFLECTION:
Intermission

PROCESSIONAL:
"We Shall Go Up with Joy" (Ps. 121, Antiphon I),
Twenty-Four Psalms and a Canticle, p. 42.

PRAYER OF BLESSING OVER GIFTS:
God our Father, be pleased to accept
the offering of this bread and wine.
They are very simple, very fragile gifts
and so truly reflect our lives
which we hope to live in a meaningful manner.
Bless our bread.
Be with us as we pray and strengthen us
so that we might have joy and hope
in you and in one another.
We ask this in Jesus' name,
who with you and the Holy Spirit,
lives as God, forever and ever.

THE TABLE PRAYER

PREFACE:
It is right to give the Lord our God thanks and praise
for we are glad and remember
that he is here among us.
God our Father, we owe you praise and thanksgiving,
for through Jesus, your Son, you have taught us
that the meaning of life here is living for others.
We could not have known this if he had not shown

that he was the way of love and total service
and that by our love of others we would be fulfilling
our lives as men and as your sons and daughters.
Therefore, Heavenly Father,
strengthened by your Spirit, dwelling within us,
we ask that you hear our voices
as we rejoice in your goodness:

HYMN OF PRAISE:
"Holy, Holy, Holy! Lord God Almighty," third verse, People's
Mass Book, #184.

ACCLAMATION AT CONSECRATION:
190b, *People's Mass Book.*

ENDING ACCLAMATION:
"Praise to the Lord," *People's Mass Book*, #175.

THE SERVICE OF COMMUNION

THE "OUR FATHER"

RITE OF PEACE

FRACTION RITE:
Litany of the "Lamb of God"

SONG:
"Wisdom Has Built Herself A House" (Antiphon I), *People's
Mass Book*, #172.

PERIOD OF REFLECTION:
Intermission

THE DISMISSAL RITE

PRAYER OF BENEDICTION:
Our Father, we thank you
for the comfort of your Son's Word,

the nourishment of his bread.
Being honest with you and with ourselves,
 we fear that we will lose heart
 in times to come.
Yet, give us the courage
 to always rise up again
 and to continually seek your will.
By our faith in your love for us
 may our way be a bit smoother,
 our lives a little calmer.
We ask this in Jesus' name,
 who with you and the Holy Spirit,
 lives as God, forever and ever.

BLESSING AND DISMISSAL

ANNOUNCEMENTS

RECESSIONAL:
 Same as Processional, third verse.

SECOND SUNDAY AFTER EPIPHANY II

Theme: The Marriage Feast of Cana

Repeat the liturgy for this Sunday in Year I, using the optional First Reading and Response (to the Gospel) not used last year.

THIRD SUNDAY AFTER EPIPHANY II

Theme: The Unity of God's People

THE ENTRANCE RITE

INVITATION TO WORSHIP:

Whenever Christians worship, the theme is unity. It is always
unity—because the whole meaning of Jesus' teaching—his
Gospel preached to the poor, his freedom pledged to captive
people—the whole meaning of his dying and being raised, is
the overcoming of barriers, of walls, and the liberating of
people into a common freedom. Jesus desires to make us of
one mind, to make us free. But we resist. We resist so much,
so consistently, that even in our worship (where the theme
is always unity) we are in fact divided. So the Church, the
sign of human oneness, is itself as fragmented, as fiercely
tribal, as any group of primitives could be. Can we rise above
our protective barriers, the differences of our made-up minds,
for just a moment now, to celebrate the commonness we
have from God? Can we reflect, even for a moment, the clear
light of God's love we have been celebrating since Christmas?
Can we pray that we make our unity real in the flesh and
blood of our lives—and our churches?

PROCESSIONAL:

"The Church's One Foundation," *People's Mass Book,* #223.

GREETING:

Grace be yours, and peace, from Almighty God
   through our reconciling Savior,
   in the Spirit of unity.
Brothers, whatever separates us is not of God,
   whatever unites us is of God.
Which do we seek, as we gather together,
   as we open ourselves to one another,
   in his presence?

PRAYER OF INVOCATION:

Mindful that God calls us to share life and love

and not live in a vacuum, let us pray:
O God, the common Father
of common daughters and common sons;
God, whose pentecostal grace makes unity
our present life and yet our goal,
we pray for peace and all that makes for peace.
We pray for love
that suffers and embraces without wounding;
for breadth and understanding to see
that there are ways other than our own;
for the will to share what we possess
with all the human family.
We pray for courage to overcome the barriers
which we and our ancestors have built.
We pray in the name of Jesus,
who with you and the Holy Spirit,
lives as God, forever and ever.

THE SERVICE OF THE WORD

FIRST READING:
Philippians 2:1–11.

RESPONSE:
Silent reflection on the following passage which should be
printed on the program: *The Little Prince*, beginning with
"I cannot play with you" to "But you will sit a little closer
to me every day," p. 65 to p. 67. Excerpt just those lines that
pertain to "taming."

SECOND READING:
1 Corinthians 12:12–14, 27.

GOSPEL ACCLAMATION:
"Alleluia, The Strife Is O'er," third verse, *People's Mass Book*,
#34.

THE GOSPEL:
Luke 1:1–4; 4:14–21.

GOSPEL ACCLAMATION:
Repeat from above.

HOMILY

GENERAL INTENTIONS:
(*Response:* O Lord, hear our prayer.)
For the whole human family, called by the Gospel to an
ever deeper and more perfect unity, we pray to the Lord:
For all those we have excluded and for whom we have
not cared enough, that Jesus' reconciling love may be no
longer smothered by our selfishness, we pray to the Lord:
For all the poor, the sick and suffering, the imprisoned and
oppressed, that the burdens they have borne alone may be
lightened and their sorrows cheered by our joining them
with our resources, work and concern, we pray to the Lord:
For all churches and their ministers, that we might better
serve as we are meant to serve, as signs and instruments
of human unity, we pray to the Lord:

PERIOD OF REFLECTION:
Intermission

PROCESSIONAL:
"Bring to the Lord Your Offerings," (Ps. 28, Antiphon III),
Twenty-Four Psalms and a Canticle, p. 15.

PRAYER OF BLESSING OVER GIFTS:
Accept, Father, this offering of bread and wine
which we give to you in thanksgiving
for all that you have taught us
through your Son, Jesus.
By these gifts provide us with the strength
to break down those barriers
which divide us and keep us
from acting as your one people.
We ask this in the name of Jesus
who with you and the Holy Spirit,
lives as God, forever and ever.

THE TABLE PRAYER

PREFACE:
"Eucharistic Prayer of Human Unity," *The Experimental Liturgy Book*, p. 100.

HYMN OF PRAISE:
"Holy, Holy, Holy! Lord God Almighty," *People's Mass Book*, #184.

ACCLAMATION AT CONSECRATION:
#235a, *People's Mass Book*.

ENDING ACCLAMATION:
#108b, *People's Mass Book*.

THE SERVICE OF COMMUNION

THE "OUR FATHER"

RITE OF PEACE

FRACTION RITE:
Litany of the "Lamb of God"

SONG:
"My Shepherd Is The Lord" (Ps. 22, Antiphon III), *Twenty-Four Psalms and a Canticle*, p. 10.

PERIOD OF REFLECTION:
Intermission

THE DISMISSAL RITE

PRAYER OF BENEDICTION:
Now in Christ Jesus,
  we who used to be so far apart
  have been brought very close.
For Jesus is the peace between us

and has broken down the barrier
which used to keep us apart.
In his own person he killed the hostility among us
and came to bring the good news of peace.
Through him we have, in one Spirit,
our way to come to you, our Father.
All praise to you,
for sending your Son among us;
may you be blessed now and forever and ever.

BLESSING AND DISMISSAL

ANNOUNCEMENTS

RECESSIONAL:
"They'll Know We Are Christians," *Hymnal for Young
Christians,* p. 132.

FOURTH SUNDAY AFTER EPIPHANY II

Theme: A Time for Gentleness

THE ENTRANCE RITE

INVITATION TO WORSHIP:
Reader: As we near the end of the Church's celebration of the
Season of Light, we pause to consider the times in which
we live. Amid all the searching, the turmoil of the day, the
cries of leaders taking men one direction and then another
—perhaps in the midst of all this we need a bit of gentleness.
Let us prepare our hearts for this celebration with the
following words:
We are a people who have walked in darkness but have
now seen a great light; upon us who have dwelt in a land
of deep shadows a light has shone. For to us a child is born,
to us a son is given.
(Adapted from Isaiah 9:1,6).
All: "Song of Christmas," *Listen to Love,* p. 44.

PROCESSIONAL:
"Praise the Lord of Heaven," *People's Mass Book,* #180.

GREETING:
Eucharistic Liturgies, p. 160.

PRAYER OF INVOCATION:
Eucharistic Liturgies, p. 160. Omit first sentence. Begin second
with address, "Father."

THE SERVICE OF THE WORD

FIRST READING:
Zephaniah 2:3, 3:12–13. Reader continues with the following:
Isaiah, the prophet, speaks of the Messiah who is to come
and foretells that he will not come as a conquering and
boisterous king but as a quiet man, a person of peace and

46

gentleness. Let us respond with the words which the prophet speaks in the name of God.

RESPONSE:
Isaiah 42:1–4.

SECOND READING:
1 Corinthians 12:31–13:13.

RESPONSE:
"Alleluia, The Strife Is O'er," *People's Mass Book,* #34. Sing only "Alleluia! Alleluia! Alleluia!" Then read "Lord God, this is the day you have made," *Your Word Is Near,* p. 47. Then repeat, "Alleluia! Alleluia! Alleluia!"

THE GOSPEL:
Matthew 5:1–12a.

GOSPEL ACCLAMATION:
Repeat "Alleluia! Alleluia! Alleluia!" from above.

HOMILY

GENERAL INTENTIONS:
(*Response:* Lord, hear our prayer.)
For those who lead us in all areas of our lives that they be mindful of the human feelings and needs of the people who look to them for leadership, let us pray to the Lord:
For those who seek change, a different way of doing things —that they not be forgetful of the difficulty of leaving the past behind; that they recognize the contribution of the past which makes the present so possible, let us pray to the Lord:
For young people who serve our country in varied fashion— the military, the Peace Corps, Vista volunteers, the college student, and those working in the labor force; for all our young people, let us pray to the Lord:
For ourselves, that by our gentleness we might encourage those who are fainthearted, give strength to those who

dream and hope, and give comfort to those who mourn,
let us pray to the Lord:

PERIOD OF REFLECTION:
Intermission

PROCESSIONAL:
"Sion, Sing," *People's Mass Book,* #165.

PRAYER OF BLESSING OVER GIFTS:
God, our Father, look upon these gifts
of bread and wine which your people offer to you
in praise and thanksgiving.
Grant that we might continue
to seek your will in all things
and be a source of light and peace
to all men who look upon us and hear our words.
This we ask in the name of Jesus, your Son,
who with you and the Holy Spirit,
lives as God, forever and ever.

THE TABLE PRAYER

PREFACE:
Holy are you and truly blessed, Father of light,
for you have rescued us and gathered together the
remnant of your flock.
Continue with "You are Light and Wisdom itself . . ." (third
line), "Liturgy of the Lord of Light," *The Experimental
Liturgy Book,* p. 109. Lines 19–29 may be omitted.

HYMN OF PRAISE:
"Praise God, From Whom All Blessings Flow," *People's Mass
Book,* #45.

ACCLAMATION AT CONSECRATION:
"Keep in Mind," *People's Mass Book,* #145.

ENDING ACCLAMATION:
"Praise to the Lord," third verse, *People's Mass Book,* #175.

THE SERVICE OF COMMUNION

THE "OUR FATHER"

RITE OF PEACE

FRACTION RITE:
Litany of the "Lamb of God"

SONG:
"O Taste and See the Goodness of the Lord," *Psalms for Singing,* Book One, p. 14.

PERIOD OF REFLECTION:
Intermission

THE DISMISSAL RITE

PRAYER OF BENEDICTION:
Eucharistic Liturgies, p. 161.

BLESSING AND DISMISSAL

ANNOUNCEMENTS

RECESSIONAL:
"Thou Whose Almighty Word," *The Hymnal of the Protestant Episcopal Church in the United States of America,* #272.

FIFTH SUNDAY AFTER EPIPHANY II

Theme: A Prayer of Thanksgiving: Reflections on the Value of Age

THE ENTRANCE RITE

INVITATION TO WORSHIP:
Walter Lippmann in *Listen to Love*, p. 41.

PROCESSIONAL:
"Praise to the Lord," *People's Mass Book*, #175.

GREETING:
Peace and blessings to you
    from our Lord Jesus Christ,
    who has revealed to us
    the love of God our Father for us.

PRAYER OF INVOCATION:
"O God, you are our origin and Father," *Your Word Is Near*,
p. 104.

THE SERVICE OF THE WORD

FIRST READING:
Job 7:1–4, 6–7.

RESPONSE:
Michael Harrington in *Listen to Love*, p. 331.

SECOND READING:
1 Corinthians 9:16–19, 22–23.

GOSPEL ACCLAMATION:
"All Men on Earth," *People's Mass Book*, #36.

THE GOSPEL:
Matthew 5:13–16.

GOSPEL ACCLAMATION:
Repeat from above.

HOMILY

GENERAL INTENTIONS:
Selection from *Your Word Is Near*, p. 30 and top of page 113.

PERIOD OF REFLECTION:
Intermission

PROCESSIONAL:
"How Can I Repay the Lord for His Goodness to Me?" (Ps. 115, Antiphon III), *Twenty-Four Psalms and a Canticle*, p. 37.

PRAYER OF BLESSING OVER GIFTS:
God, our Father, be pleased to accept
these gifts of bread and wine
which we offer to you together
with the prayer of your Son, Jesus.
In return, fill us with your own friendship and life.
This we ask in Jesus' name,
who with you and the Holy Spirit,
is living as God, forever and ever.

THE TABLE PRAYER

PREFACE:
"The Canon of the Pilgrim Church," *The Experimental Liturgy Book*, p. 73.

HYMN OF PRAISE:
"Holy, Holy, Holy" from *The English-Latin Sacramentary* (spoken).

ACCLAMATION AT CONSECRATION:
#235a, *People's Mass Book*.

ENDING ACCLAMATION:
#190b, *People's Mass Book*.

THE SERVICE OF COMMUNION

THE "OUR FATHER"

RITE OF PEACE

FRACTION RITE:
Litany of the "Lamb of God"

SONG:
"Behold Among Men," *Biblical Hymns and Psalms,* p. 36.

PERIOD OF REFLECTION:
Intermission

THE DISMISSAL RITE

PRAYER OF BENEDICTION:
"We have heard your Word, O God," *Your Word Is Near,*
p. 123.

BLESSING AND DISMISSAL

ANNOUNCEMENTS

RECESSIONAL:
"The Church's One Foundation," *People's Mass Book,* #223.

SIXTH SUNDAY AFTER EPIPHANY II

Theme: Grateful Praise to the Father for His Mercy

THE ENTRANCE RITE

INVITATION TO WORSHIP:

In just a few hours, we will begin another season of salvation
—Lent. Today we prepare for that time when we will sift
through ourselves to see what does and what does not need
change. Or as T. S. Eliot says in his poem, "Ash Wednesday,"
it is the time when we pray: "Teach us to care and not to
care."

Today we pray about our general need for conversion and
specifically our need for mercy and understanding with each
other; for this is what opens us to God's mercy, which is what
Lent is all about. Woodrow Wilson once said. (Here insert
p. 212, *Listen to Love*.) It is this spirit of openness to the
worth and trust of another, this "mercifulness" for which we
pray.

PROCESSIONAL:

"Rise Up, O Men Of God," *The Hymnal of the Protestant
Episcopal Church in the United States of America*, #535.

GREETING:

We call upon the Lord and he hears us;
in our need for mercy and our need to be merciful,
may his peace and blessings be ours in abundance.

PRAYER OF INVOCATION:

"God, you are not happy with us," *Your Word Is Near*, p. 131.
Introduce with "Recalling that we do need to be more trusting
and merciful to each other, let us pray:"

THE SERVICE OF THE WORD

FIRST READING:

Samuel 26:2,7–9, 12–13, 22–23. (In verse 22, read "David
called out" instead of "David answered."

RESPONSE:

(Reflection on the following passage which should be printed on program.)
From the reading about David and Saul and from the following selection from the writings of Miguel de Unamuno, the Spanish philospher, we see that reconciliation and justice are not served by killing, but by the unity of living beings, by openness and trust. (Here print quote from Miguel de Unamuno in *Listen to Love*, p. 214.)

SECOND READING:

Dietrich Bonhoeffer in *Listen to Love*, p. 53. Introduction: The Second Reading today is from the German Lutheran pastor, Dietrich Bonhoeffer. Here he speaks of the trust so necessary for happiness and peace; he speaks of the trust he learned while in prison, in the midst of mistrust.

GOSPEL ACCLAMATION:

"Alleluia! Alleluia," *Biblical Hymns and Psalms*, Vol. II, p. 88; sung before and after these lines:
Sow freely, Lord God, the seed of your Word over
   the world;
   that we be able to grow and live according to
   the mind and Spirit of Jesus the Lord.

THE GOSPEL:

Luke 6:27–38.

GOSPEL ACCLAMATION:

Repeat "Alleluia! Alleluia!" from above.

HOMILY

GENERAL INTENTIONS:

(Response: O Lord, give strength but make us gentle.)
For a spirit of compassion in the hearts of all men
   seeking to convert their lives as Christian people,
   let us pray to the Lord:
For the victims of violence and crime that their

faith in the God of mercy may not be weakened,
let us pray to the Lord:
For the revolutionaries in our society, that they
may never resort to violence in their frustration and attempts
at reform, let us pray to the Lord:
For those we sometimes take for granted—those who serve
us in many different ways, but do their jobs quietly and
without thanks, let us pray to the Lord:

PERIOD OF REFLECTION:
Intermisson

PROCESSIONAL:
"All the Earth Proclaim the Lord," *People's Mass Book*, #141.

PRAYER OF BLESSING OVER GIFTS:
Father, we are ready to become your people,
to approach you through your Son, Jesus Christ.
We present these gifts as signs of ourselves.
By our faith and your promise
they and we can be transformed
into the sign of your presence.
Make us then, a new people, able to share your mercy
wherever men are hurt.
We pray in the name of Jesus your Son,
who with the Spirit lives with you
forever and ever.

THE TABLE PRAYER

PREFACE:
First sentence of "Eucharistic Prayer of Human Unity," *The
Experimental Liturgy Book*, p. 100. Continue with the
following:
We praise and thank you for calling us through faith
to share your gift of love with the world
and strengthening us to turn
from selfishness and pride.
In sending your Son to be one of us,

you have given light to our world
and we want to walk in this light;
we want to meet you in the loving service
of our fellow man
even if this demands a sacrifice.
We thank you for accepting us as we are
and once more offering your love to us
as nourishment and strength.
With all of creation, we join the chorus of praise,
singing together:

HYMN OF PRAISE:
"Holy, Holy, Holy! Lord God Almighty," second verse,
People's Mass Book, #184.

ACCLAMATION AT CONSECRATION:
#190b, *People's Mass Book*.

ENDING ACCLAMATION:
"You Alone Are Holy," *Biblical Hymns and Psalms*, Vol. II,
p. 52.

THE SERVICE OF COMMUNION

THE "OUR FATHER"

RITE OF PEACE

FRACTION RITE:
Litany of the "Lamb of God"

SONG:
"God Is Love," *Hymnal for Young Christians*, p. 95.

PERIOD OF REFLECTION:
Intermission
Reading for Meditation (*printed on program*):
We must forgive those who trespass against us. These words
of Jesus cause us embarrassment. We tend to do the opposite,

insisting on our rights and being unforgiving. Yet Jesus is the embodiment of love; we have just taken this love as food. He is the forgiveness of sin, and perfect justice for the world. Where do I need to reflect this same love and forgiveness in my world? (Adapted from *Your Word Is Near*, p. 134.)

THE DISMISSAL RITE

PRAYER OF BENEDICTION:
    "You have forgiven us," *Your Word Is Near*, p. 136.

BLESSING AND DISMISSAL

ANNOUNCEMENTS

RECESSIONAL:
    "Priestly People," *People's Mass Book*, #146.

ASH WEDNESDAY II

Theme: "I Shall Arise and Return to My Father"

THE ENTRANCE RITE

INVITATION TO WORSHIP:
"Confessions at the Empty Tomb," *Interrobang*, p. 80.

PROCESSION:
The reader starts the fire. As the ministers arrive, they place
the palms they are carrying in the fire. People are singing,
"Have Mercy On Me" (Ps. 50, Antiphon I), *Twenty-Four
Psalms and a Canticle*, p. 22.

GREETING AND PRAYER OF INVOCATION:
My friends in faith, we gather today
    to make a new beginning,
    to make a prayer of thanksgiving to the Father
    for his patience and his mercy.
For even though we sometimes turn our backs
    to him and to one another,
    he remains always faithful,
    calling us back to live together.
Today he speaks to us in his Son,
    and so we come here confident
    that he will welcome us.
With deep sorrow for our failures in the past,
    let us turn to him now in prayer:
Father, we stand before you now,
    relieved and at peace because of your presence.
In times past we have made our lives
    barren and desert-like,
    but your merciful kindness has brought us to life
    time and time again.
By the waters of baptism we were first brought to life;
    through our efforts this Lent, may we be able
    to leave behind, once and for all,

whatever is contrary to your Son's life;
so that when the Easter breaks upon us,
we may blossom into your life,
ever to be with you and your Son,
in peace and joy, living together forever and ever.

THE SERVICE OF THE WORD

FIRST READING:
Joel 1:13–20.

RESPONSE:
Micah 7:7–9; 16–18.

THE GOSPEL:
Matthew 9:1–13.

RESPONSE:
Blessing of the Ashes. Use *The English-Latin Sacramentary*
prayer of blessing of ashes, beginning, "You desire not the
death but the repentance of sinners." Preface with: "Let us
pray to God to have pity as we humbly accept this sign of
penance."

PROCESSION:
People place an altar bread in specified container as they
come forward to receive ashes—"this mark of your determined
conversion." All sing, "Yes, I Shall Arise," *People's Mass Book*,
#174.

PRAYER OF BLESSING OVER GIFTS:
Only the "Let us pray that my sacrifice and yours be
acceptable . . ." is used today.

THE TABLE PRAYER

PREFACE:
Therefore, God our Father, we give you
the praise belonging to you,

for by sending your Son to be one of us,
you have adopted us as your people.
But being human we quickly and easily forget you.
Now with your whole Church
we begin our pilgrimage back to you
so that through the death experience in our bodies
by fasting,
through listening to your Word,
we are urged on to greater service of love.
By trying to put on the attitude of Jesus
we will all be able to celebrate his resurrection
as our own.
You now send your Spirit among us
to put us on the path to peace,
so that we do not rely on our own power
or follow the wrong path
but follow only your Son, the lamp to our feet.
With all of your people and with all creation
groaning for a springtime of renewal,
we praise you, saying together with one voice:

HYMN OF PRAISE:
(*Spoken*) "Holy, Holy, Holy" from *The English-Latin Sacramentary.*

ACCLAMATION AT CONSECRATION:
#235a, *People's Mass Book.*

ENDING ACCLAMATION:
#108b, *People's Mass Book.*

THE SERVICE OF COMMUNION

THE "OUR FATHER"

RITE OF PEACE

FRACTION RITE:
Litany of the "Lamb of God"

SONG:
"Whatsoever You Do," *People's Mass Book,* #208.

PERIOD OF REFLECTION:
Intermission

THE DISMISSAL RITE

PRAYER OF BENEDICTION:
Eucharistic Liturgies, p. 21.

BLESSING AND DISMISSAL

ANNOUNCEMENTS

RECESSIONAL:
"Now Thank We All Our God," *People's Mass Book,* #178.

FIRST SUNDAY OF LENT II

Theme: Freedom of Christian Poverty

THE ENTRANCE RITE

INVITATION TO WORSHIP:
A *New Catechism*, page 435, through "and this is an endless process."

PROCESSIONAL:
"Thou Whose Almighty Word," *The Hymnal of the Protestant Episcopal Church in the United States of America*, #272.

GREETING:
God our Father, in his loving kindness, has shared with us
the life-giving gift of his Son, Jesus.
May their Spirit be with us and show us
the freedom and wealth to be found
in our loving service and concern for one another.

PENITENTIAL RITE:
As we gather to celebrate the Lord's Supper, we are aware
of our own poverty and the poverty which ours causes among
our brothers. Let us honestly admit our faults with the purpose
of converting to the way of our Lord Jesus.
Because we are tempted to place excessive dependence and
stamps of excellence on those who possess wealth, power
and social status, and strive to achieve our happiness by
attaining the same goals, let us pray to the Lord:
Because of those attitudes in ourselves which cause us to
neglect our brother's needs until we are first fully satisfied,
let us pray to the Lord:
Because we cannot, at times, honestly admit our own needs
and so disguise our poverty by isolating ourselves from
others and refusing to call upon others for help, let us pray
to the Lord:
The celebrant ends each petition by saying, "Lord have

mercy"; the people respond by singing the same response, according to any simple melody chosen by the music director.

PRAYER OF INVOCATION:
God our Father, we look about and see
    all that man can accomplish,
    all that he can do to bring himself peace and contentment.
And yet we are not content.
We seek something else, Father, and have an inkling
    that you and your Son's Word
    contain the end of our yearnings.
We pray now, though fearful of what the words might mean,
    that by hearing his Word we may find the truth
    which offers us the joy and peace of life
    which we so eagerly desire.
Be with us as we pray in Jesus' name,
    who with you and the Holy Spirit, is living as God,
    forever and ever.

THE SERVICE OF THE WORD

FIRST READING:
Ecclesiasticus 3:30(33)–31(34); 4:1–5, 8–11.

RESPONSE:
Ecclesiasticus 29:8(11)–12(15); 4:10.

SECOND READING:
James 2:14–24; 26.

RESPONSE:
Two minutes' silent reflection.

GOSPEL ACCLAMATION:
"Grant to Us" (Jer. 31:31–34), *Biblical Hymns and Psalms*, p. 40.

THE GOSPEL:
Luke 12:13–15; 22–34.

GOSPEL ACCLAMATION:
    Repeat from above.

HOMILY

GENERAL INTENTIONS:
    (*Response:* Lord, teach us to spend ourselves in love.)
    For those who are caught in the vicious cycle of poverty,
        that they may find concern and assistance to help themselves
        from those who call themselves Christian, let us pray to
        the Lord:
    That each man might seek to realize all of his capabilities
        and so be of ever-increasing service to the Christian
        community and the community of man, let us pray to the
        Lord:
    That those who are rich in material possessions be not
        despised nor neglected; that they may be regarded by
        God's people not just as sources of money and power but
        also as people having human needs and wants, let us pray
        to the Lord:
    For ourselves, that we be honest with ourselves in admitting
        our own poverty and, in seeking assistance from others,
        discover the ability to be concerned for others, let us pray
        to the Lord:
    That the Church, God's holy people, never become so
        concerned with maintaining material holdings, that we
        forget that we are to be a people believing in, and living
        as, One who came as a poor man to serve all men in their
        poverty, let us pray to the Lord:

PERIOD OF REFLECTION:
    Intermission

PROCESSIONAL:
    "My Shepherd Is the Lord" (Ps. 22, Antiphon I), *Twenty-Four
    Psalms and a Canticle*, p. 10.

PRAYER OF BLESSING OVER GIFTS:
    To you, Father of all goodness,

we offer our bread and our wine,
poor gifts indeed and so
truly representative of ourselves.
By your power transform these gifts
and make us prosper in your own divine Life.
This we ask in Jesus' name,
who with you and the Holy Spirit,
is living as God, forever and ever.

THE TABLE PRAYER

PREFACE:
It is right, Lord and Father, that we look to you
and offer you the praise belonging to you.
While you have clothed us with dignity
and called us your people,
we have often denied your Word.
We have fallen and feel, very often,
that we can go no farther.
Sustained, however, by the faith of your Church,
we come to you,
for you heal us and strengthen us
for the sake of your mercy
expressed in Jesus, our brother.
We are confident that you will lavish your strength upon us
and we praise you.
With all of creation awaiting a springtime of renewal,
we thank you, singing together:

HYMN OF PRAISE:
"Holy, Holy, Holy! Lord God Almighty," *People's Mass Book,*
#184.

ACCLAMATION AT CONSECRATION:
"Keep in Mind," *People's Mass Book,* #145.

ENDING ACCLAMATION:
#190b, *People's Mass Book.*

THE SERVICE OF COMMUNION

THE "OUR FATHER"

RITE OF PEACE

FRACTION RITE:
Litany of the "Lamb of God"

SONG:
"Whatsoever You Do," *People's Mass Book,* #208.

PERIOD OF REFLECTION:
Intermission

THE DISMISSAL RITE

PRAYER OF BENEDICTION:
God our Father, we thank you for the gift of your Son,
in his Bread, in his Word, in his very Person.
He is ever with us, if only we have eyes to see;
he ever speaks to us,
if only we have ears to hear.
Give us new eyes and new ears
to see his presence and to hear his call
in the men and women in need who touch our lives.
May we have the courage to spend ourselves
where Jesus leads us
and thus give you praise and glory
on earth and in the life to come,
forever and ever.
(Adapted from *Eucharistic Liturgies,* p. 24.)

BLESSING AND DISMISSAL

ANNOUNCEMENTS

RECESSIONAL:
"They'll Know We Are Christians," *Hymnal for Young Christians,* p. 132.

SECOND SUNDAY OF LENT II

Theme: God's Action—Man's Reaction

THE ENTRANCE RITE

INVITATION TO WORSHIP:
Dag Hammarksjold in *The Underground Mass Book*, p. 57.

PROCESSIONAL:
"These Forty Days of Lent," verses 1 and 3, *People's Mass Book*, #21.

GREETING:
Eucharistic Liturgies, p. 25.

PENITENTIAL RITE:
My brothers and sisters in the Lord, as we prepare to share in this supper of the Lord, let us first of all call to mind our sinfulness so that we may seek to change and to pattern our lives after the life of our Lord, Jesus.
Priest: In sorrow for the times we have neglected to open our hearts and our doors to those who suffer in their body and in their mind, we pray to the Lord:
Response: Lord, have mercy (*sung according to any simple melody known to congregation*).
Priest: In sorrow for the times we have failed to confess with our words and our works, that Christ dwells within us, we pray to the Lord:
Response: Christ, have mercy.
Priest: In sorrow for the times we have prayed for God's help, and then refused to be reconciled to God's answer, we pray to the Lord:
Response: Lord, have mercy.

PRAYER OF INVOCATION:
God our Father, in your loving kindness
you have reached out and touched us;
you have sought to hold us close
as a mother clings to her child.

Yet, we have often pulled away from your loving gestures.
Change us now, by the power of your Son's Word,
  so that we may renew with you
  a friendship strained or broken by our stubbornness.
Let us reach out and touch you in each event,
  in each person who shares our life.
All this we ask in the name of Jesus,
  who with you and the Holy Spirit,
  is living as God, forever and ever.

THE SERVICE OF THE WORD

FIRST READING:
Genesis 15:5–12; 17–18.

RESPONSE:
Psalm 27: 1, 7, 8b–9, followed by a brief period of meditation.

SECOND READING:
Omitted today.

GOSPEL ACCLAMATION:
"Grant to Us" (Jer. 31:31–34), *Biblical Hymns and Psalms*,
p. 40.

THE GOSPEL:
Luke 9:28–36.

GOSPEL ACCLAMATION:
Repeat from above.

HOMILY

GENERAL INTENTIONS:
(*Response:* O Lord, hear our prayer.)
For the men and women of today, that in their joys,
  their hopes, their griefs and their anxieties, they make a
  covenant with God and rely on his love, we pray to the
  Lord:

For members of this community, that as they reflect on the
world of today, they may be led to take a real share in
the struggles and hopes of their fellow men, we pray to
the Lord:

For ourselves, that during this season of Lent, we be less
hypocritical and earnestly seek an internal renewal and
reformation leading us to become more sincere followers of
Christ, we pray to the Lord:

PERIOD OF REFLECTION:
Intermission

PROCESSIONAL:
"We Gather Together," *People's Mass Book*, #53.

PRAYER OF BLESSING OVER GIFTS:
Father, you are most generous
in that you care for each of us.
We wish to give you thanks and praise
because of all your goodness toward us.
Accept these gifts of bread and wine
as our offering of gratitude.
May they be pleasing to you
as they are joined with the gift of your Son,
Jesus Christ our Lord, who with you and the Holy Spirit,
is living as God, forever and ever.

THE TABLE PRAYER

PREFACE:
Lord God, Almighty Father, we come before you,
speaking your praises and giving you our thanksgiving.
When we have denied your love or doubted your words,
you have remained steadfast
in your loving kindness toward us.
You cannot bear it when we destroy each other,
and so you come to us constantly
to break the cycle of evil and deception
that holds us captive.

You are present in Jesus your Son
  so that we walk in his light
  and find you as the firm ground under our feet.
You live only for us;
  you are our Father in the greatness of your love;
  and so with all your people
  we praise you, singing together:
(Adapted from Huub Oosterhuis, *Your Word Is Near*, pp.
131 and 134.)

HYMN OF PRAISE:
  "O God, Almighty Father," *Our Parish Prays and Sings,* #12.

ACCLAMATION AT CONSECRATION:
  #190b, *People's Mass Book.*

ENDING ACCLAMATION:
  #108b, *People's Mass Book.*

THE SERVICE OF COMMUNION

THE "OUR FATHER"

RITE OF PEACE

FRACTION RITE:
  Litany of the "Lamb of God"

SONG:
  "My Soul Is Waiting For the Lord" (Ps. 130, Antiphon II),
  Biblical Hymns and Psalms, p. 104.

PERIOD OF REFLECTION:
  Intermission

THE DISMISSAL RITE

PRAYER OF BENEDICTION:
  Eucharistic Liturgies, p. 26.

BLESSING AND DISMISSAL

ANNOUNCEMENTS

RECESSIONAL:
Same as Processional, fourth verse.

THIRD SUNDAY OF LENT II

Theme: The Spirit of Christian Giving

THE ENTRANCE RITE

INVITATION TO WORSHIP:
(Introduce the following reading with six or seven current newspaper headlines relating seemingly senseless tragedies.) Such are the headlines that greet us day after day. Jesus dealt with senseless, cruel casualties like those in war and accidents more than once in his lifetime. He ended the same way himself—the way of madness, when he was at the height of his powers. From an overall look, life does make sense, but it didn't make a great deal more sense for Jesus than it does for the innocent victims around the globe today or yesterday. The season of Lent, though, gives a little light on the whole life Jesus lived. Life with Jesus is an everyday business, with horror, tragedy, sadness. And the transfiguration which we heard last Sunday in the Gospel is a kind of "curtain-raiser" on all the blooming, bursting life and glory to come. Voices from bright clouds don't happen to us every day. So something else will have to make a change in us like the change in the apostles at the transfiguration. Until that change happens in us, senseless things, evil things will keep on happening. Jesus is here to change us, help us figure things out—we need to listen to him, doing things more on his terms than just our own. We need a turning point in our lives, like the one Jesus had at the transfiguration. If we haven't had this, then we've got to keep working until the day when something hits us and we understand that all the tragedy, sickness, sorrow does make sense, and that we can do something about it. Then we will be transfigured—life will make much more sense after all. It is this Lenten effort to be transformed that our liturgy is all about today.

PROCESSIONAL:
"These Forty Days of Lent," *People's Mass Book,* #21.

GREETING:

Blessings and grace to you who have come
for deeper understanding and conviction;
you who have come for the grace
to root all parts of your lives in Jesus
and so to transform not only yourselves
but also those who touch our lives.
May the spirit of the transfigured Lord be with you.

PENITENTIAL RITE:

(*Response:* Lord, have mercy.)
For relying more on our own strengths than on the presence
of God; for following our own ways and keeping our
distance from the ways of Christ, we ask for forgiveness
and pray to the Lord:
For our forgetfulness of others; for not providing what each
of us needs most—affection, generosity, faithfulness, we
ask forgiveness and pray to the Lord:
For not bearing our share in the struggle to live, preach and
provide for the Gospel, we ask forgiveness and pray to
the Lord:

PRAYER OF INVOCATION:

Lord God, as a miracle of humanity and love,
as a Word that makes people free,
your Son has come to us as servant,
showing that he belonged to you alone,
and not even death could hold him.
We pray that he may come to life among us here,
that we may not be ensnared in discord and doubt,
or filled with self-centeredness;
but that we may give ourselves totally
to you in every way, as did Jesus.
It is in his name that we offer this prayer,
now and forever and ever.
(Adapted from "Lord God, as a miracle of humanity and
love," *Your Word Is Near*, p. 60.)

THE SERVICE OF THE WORD

FIRST READING:
Philippians 3:17–21.

RESPONSE:
Lord God, you remind me that I shall be transformed as
was your Son, if I bear my share of the struggle which the
Gospel entails; you have also reminded me that he who sows
sparingly will also reap sparingly. You, Lord, are able to
provide me with every blessing in abundance, for you who
supply seed to the farmer and bread for food will supply
and multiply my resources and increase my harvest. May
I glorify you, O God, by my obedience in acknowledging
your Gospel and by the generosity of my gifts for my fellow
Christians and all others. I need not be reminded of your
Son, Jesus Christ, who though rich, for our sake became poor.
He is your beloved Son, and you bid us to hear him and
follow his way. Give us this strength.
(Adapted from 2 Corinthians 9:6–15.)

SECOND READING:
Omitted today.

THE GOSPEL:
Mark 9:9, 14–29.

HOMILY

PROFESSION OF FAITH:
The Apostles' Creed

GENERAL INTENTIONS:
    (*Response:* Lord, make us aware of our duties.)
    Let us pray—and let us do even more than pray—for our
       diocese, for the success of its endeavors of service, for
       everyone with whom we are associated in the Church's
       work, let us pray to the Lord:
    For all who work in the missions of our diocese, let us pray
       to the Lord:
    For the people all around us, whose lives are difficult and

troubled, and whose suffering is unseen, let us pray to the Lord:

For those who can no longer find meaning or purpose in their lives, those who have turned from faith and have lost themselves by and through excessive drink or drugs, let us pray to the Lord:

For those who have died—remember their names and preserve them in your love—let us pray to the Lord:

PERIOD OF REFLECTION:
Intermission

PROCESSIONAL:
"Bring to the Lord Your Offerings" (Ps. 28, Antiphon III), *Twenty-Four Psalms and a Canticle*, p. 14.

PRAYER OF BLESSING OVER GIFTS:
Father, we come before you as chosen people
    whom you love very much.
We acknowledge with sorrow our failures to live in peace,
    the mercy and kindness we have not shown,
    the love we have been unwilling to give.
We set before you now this bread and wine
    as signs that we are yours and yours alone.
Grant that whatever we do,
    we do in the name of your Son Jesus Christ,
    through whom we pray and give you glory,
    now and forever and ever.

THE TABLE PRAYER

PREFACE:
We thank you, God, our Father,
    for your loving trust in men.
In creation, you first clothed us with dignity,
    calling us not things, but sons,
    and saw that we were very good.
From the beginning it has ever been our vocation
    to fashion the world in the image of your love.

You made us not to be idle, living for ourselves,
  but to build new cities from the ground,
  sing new songs in the air,
  and make this world livable for everybody,
  not just a select few.
Today, as never before, your work is in our hands;
  during these forty days we search for ways to return to you,
  starving our selfishness,
  and trying to feed our generosity.
In all our frailty, we join now around your table,
  in love, in hesitation, in risk,
  and we offer thanks, trying to be what we truly
  are—the work of your hands and co-workers
  with your Son, Jesus Christ.
Confident that you accept us as we are,
  we join all creation in praising you,
  saying together with one voice:
(Adapted from "Canon of the Sons of God," *Eucharistic
Liturgies*, p. 194, and from "The Canon of the Pilgrim Church,"
The Experimental Liturgy Book, p. 73.)

HYMN OF PRAISE:
  "Praise God, From Whom All Blessings Flow," *People's Mass
  Book*, #45.

ACCLAMATION AT CONSECRATION:
  #190b, *People's Mass Book.*

ENDING ACCLAMATION:
  "You Alone Are Holy," *Biblical Hymns and Psalms*, Vol. II,
  p. 52.

THE SERVICE OF COMMUNION

THE "OUR FATHER"

RITE OF PEACE

FRACTION RITE:
  Litany of the "Lamb of God"

SONG:
"My Soul Is Waiting for the Lord" (Ps. 130, Antiphon I),
Biblical Hymns and Psalms, p. 104.

PERIOD OF REFLECTION:
Intermission
Reading for Meditation (*printed on program*): "Prayer
Before a Twenty-Dollar Bill," *Prayers,* p. 32.

THE DISMISSAL RITE

PRAYER OF BENEDICTION:
We thank you, Father, that you are always with us,
and that all the promises you have made
to transform this earth will come true;
yet we ask that, as we struggle
to know what you want of us,
you will show us the mind of your Son
expressed in the needs and anxieties of those around us.
Through the name of your Son we ask this,
and through him we give you all praise and glory,
now and forever and ever.

BLESSING AND DISMISSAL

ANNOUNCEMENTS

RECESSIONAL:
"They'll Know We Are Christians by Our Love," *Hymnal
for Young Christians,* p. 132.

FOURTH SUNDAY OF LENT II

Theme: Praise and Thanksgiving to the Father for the Mercy
Shown His People

THE ENTRANCE RITE

INVITATION TO WORSHIP:
Today we assemble to pray, remembering that the sin of
Adam, repeated by us with every selfishness, is a separation,
a breaking up of man from man and man from God. God
has continually been at work in the world reconciling all
men, not allowing our house to remain divided against itself.
He made alliances with Abraham, Moses and David, preparing
a people for the coming of one who could crush the head
of division and pride, who would gather the broken fragments
of Adam and forge them into a new and far greater
reconciliation than we had ever known.
Today we remember that Jesus reconciles us with the Father
and feeds us with his Word and his very self for strength
to be reconciled with each other. From the first moment of
the dialogue between God and man, God knew the weakness
of man; he knew that despite all his testimonies of love and
fidelity, man would draw back and prefer to take a path
that seemed easier.
This morning, then, we gather to pray, to profess that we
have sinned, but that we shall arise and go back to our Father.
We do this with Jesus Christ in our midst.

PROCESSIONAL:
"My Soul Is Longing for Your Peace" (Ps. 131), *Biblical
Hymns and Psalms*, p. 98.

GREETING:
Eucharistic Liturgies, p. 31.

PENITENTIAL RITE:
Now, in silence, let us examine ourselves regarding those

78

things which keep us from our Father.
*(After a pause all are invited to join in reading the Prayer
of Invocation.)*

PRAYER OF INVOCATION:
First "Rite of Reconciliation," *The Underground Mass Book,*
p. 21.

THE SERVICE OF THE WORD

FIRST READING:
Daniel 3:34–43.

RESPONSE:
"Yes, I Shall Arise," *People's Mass Book,* #174.

SECOND READING:
1 Corinthians 5:17–21.

RESPONSE:
"Who should we be, O Lord," *Your Word Is Near,* p. 133.

GOSPEL ACCLAMATION:
"Yes, I Shall Arise," cited in Response above.

THE GOSPEL:
Luke 15:1–3, 11–32.

GOSPEL ACCLAMATION:
Repeat from above.

HOMILY

GENERAL INTENTIONS:
Selection from pp. 141–143, *Your Word Is Near.*
(*Response:* Lord, make us instruments of your peace.)

PERIOD OF REFLECTION:
Intermission

PROCESSIONAL:

"Come Thou, Almighty King," *The Hymnal of the Protestant Episcopal Church in the United States of America,* #271.

PRAYER OF BLESSING OVER GIFTS:

Only the "Let us pray that my sacrifice and yours . . ." with its response is used today.

THE TABLE PRAYER

PREFACE:

Father, we return to you, offering the praise belonging
    to you.
For from time beyond our imagination
    you have loved us.
When we have doubted your love or denied your Word,
    you have not sent your wrath to crush us,
    but continue to call us your sons.
You are lavish in your loving forgiveness.
When we bring to you our weaknesses and failures,
    you set before us a banquet,
    feeding us with your mercy and life,
    that we may grow to express that same attitude
    of Jesus your Son who became obedient unto death,
    even to death on a cross,
    reconciling us to you and to your world.
In thanksgiving for your Son who leads us back to you
    and prompts us to bend our selfishness into peace,
    we praise you, singing together:

HYMN OF PRAISE:

"Praise to the Lord," first verse, *People's Mass Book,* #175.

ACCLAMATION AT CONSECRATION:

#190b, *People's Mass Book.*

ENDING ACCLAMATION:

"Praise to the Lord," cited above, third verse.

THE SERVICE OF COMMUNION

THE "OUR FATHER"

RITE OF PEACE

FRACTION RITE:
Litany of the "Lamb of God"

SONG:
"O Taste and See the Goodness of the Lord," *Psalms for Singing*, Book One, p. 14.

PERIOD OF REFLECTION:
Intermission
Reading for Meditation (printed on program): "The Prayer of St. Francis," *Discovery in Prayer*, p. 99.

THE DISMISSAL RITE

PRAYER OF BENEDICTION:
"You cannot endure," *Your Word Is Near*, p. 132.

BLESSING AND DISMISSAL

ANNOUNCEMENTS

RECESSIONAL:
"Grant to Us" (Jer. 31:31–34), *Biblical Hymns and Psalms*, p. 40.

FIFTH SUNDAY OF LENT II

Theme: Grateful Praise to the Father for the Forgiveness He Promises to His People

THE ENTRANCE RITE

INVITATION TO WORSHIP:
We gather to pray. We try to turn the little three-letter word "God" into a name that means something to me—to us, now. We have to make the long journey from "God" to "Father"— a name full of echoes of his entire history with people. A name of a lover who forgives and forgets. With gratefulness for his being our Father, we affirm our brotherhood by praying a litany as our celebrant enters to preside over this Eucharist: (Adapted from *Your Word Is Near*, pp. 6–7.)

PENITENTIAL RITE:
"Litany" in *Discovery in Prayer*, p. 136 only.

PRAYER OF INVOCATION:
"We are your Church, a people on the way," *Your Word Is Near*, p. 145.

THE SERVICE OF THE WORD

FIRST READING:
Isaiah 43:16–21.

RESPONSE:
"My Soul Is Longing for Your Peace," *Biblical Hymns and Psalms*, p. 98.

SECOND READING:
Philippians 3:8–14.

RESPONSE:
Silent reflection

GOSPEL ACCLAMATION:
"If you, O Lord, should mark our sins" (Ps. 129, Antiphon
II), *Twenty-Four Psalms and a Canticle*, p. 52.

THE GOSPEL:
John 8:1–11.

GOSPEL ACCLAMATION:
Repeat from above.

HOMILY

GENERAL INTENTIONS:
(*Response:* Lord, hear our prayer.)
For those who are absent from our assembly because of illness;
for those who are facing death alone, and for those who
are frightened, let us pray to the Lord:
For those who are absent because they have been jailed
by mistake, especially for those in this condition who are
poor and cannot afford bail, that their suffering, due to the
slowness of our courts and our justice, will be lessened, let
us pray to the Lord:
For those who are away from us, fighting in war, that they
may return soon, sound of body and of mind, let us pray
to the Lord:
For those who are not here because their faith has failed,
let us pray to the Lord:

PERIOD OF REFLECTION:
Intermission

PROCESSIONAL:
"Praise the Lord, O Heavens," second verse, *People's Mass
Book*, #181.

PRAYER OF BLESSING OVER GIFTS:
Only the "Let us pray that my sacrifice and yours . . ."
with its response is used today.

THE TABLE PRAYER

PREFACE:
"The Book of Common Worship," Provisional Services, *The Experimental Liturgy Book*, p. 56. May be abbreviated by using only these lines (starting with "All glory is yours . . ."):
1–3, 6–7, 8–10, 14, 18–21.

HYMN OF PRAISE:
"Praise the Lord of Heaven," *Our Parish Prays and Sings*, #13.

ACCLAMATION AT CONSECRATION:
#235a, *People's Mass Book.*

ENDING ACCLAMATION:
#190b, *People's Mass Book.*

THE SERVICE OF COMMUNION

THE "OUR FATHER"

RITE OF PEACE

FRACTION RITE:
Litany of the "Lamb of God"

SONG:
"Peace, My Friends," *Hymnal for Young Christians*, Vol. II, p. 34.

PERIOD OF REFLECTION:
Intermission

THE DISMISSAL RITE

PRAYER OF BENEDICTION:

"Lord God, we have heard your word," *Your Word Is Near*, p. 123.

BLESSING AND DISMISSAL

ANNOUNCEMENTS

RECESSIONAL:
"Rise Up, O Men of God," *The Hymnal of the Protestant Episcopal Church in the United States of America,* #535.

PALM SUNDAY II

Theme: The Lord's Entry Into Jerusalem

THE ENTRANCE RITE AND SERVICE OF THE WORD

INVITATION TO WORSHIP:
(The celebration begins in the parish hall or in some place outside the church.)
We gather together today to recall the presence of the Lord in us by remembering his entry into Jerusalem, an entry which began in triumphant glory and moved to violent confusion a few days later—all to be finished by the triumphant resurrection of Easter.

PROCESSIONAL:
"To Jesus Christ, Our Sovereign King," *People's Mass Book,* #48.

GREETING:
Blessings and peace to you who have come in faith
to sense the presence of the Lamb of God
who has come to take away the sins of the world.

BLESSING OF THE PALMS:
Lord Jesus Christ, our King and Suffering Servant,
in your honor we carry these branches and sing
your praises.
Let your blessing, we pray you,
be in any place where these branches are carried,
so that they may remind us of the victory that will be ours
when we have tried day in and day out
to put on your attitude of service
to our world and our Father—
you who live and reign with the Father
and with us forever and ever.

(While the palms are distributed, the celebrant and people continue as indicated below.)

86

Celebrant: God and Father of our Lord Jesus Christ,
   we ask you to bless this palm
   which we are holding.
  It is a sign of victory—
   a sign that tells us your kingdom is with us,
   a sign that Jesus is King of all men,
   a sign that your Church is alive and concerned,
   a sign that our nation is a place
   dedicated to the Christian principles
   of freedom, peace, equality, and brotherhood;
   it is a sign of the world, reborn and unified
   through the coming of Jesus.
  We ask you to bless all that this sign of palm signifies
   through Jesus Christ who is with us, forever and ever.
  God and Father of our Lord Jesus Christ,
   we ask again that you bless this palm
   we are holding,
   for not only is it a sign of victory,
   it is also a sign of martyrdom and contradiction.
People: It is a sign that tells us your kingdom is still
   not complete but still very much in the slow process of
   becoming, in need of fulfillment.
  It is a sign that Jesus, proclaimed as King, was killed by
   men, a martyr for men. It is a sign that your Church
   must be killed in all the ways it spreads confusion, discord
   and alienation from the world—if it is to live.
  It is a sign that men, white or black or of any race,
   who have stood for fulfillment and continuation
   of your kingdom will always die as they have in
   these years, because of those who oppose the Word of
   your Son.
  It is a sign that shows that our nation, tormented by fears
   and riots and intolerance of the indifferent, expresses our
   dishonesty and hypocrisy.
  It is a sign of the world threatened by war, destruction,
   poverty and affluence.
  It is a sign that says both martyrdom and contradiction seem
   to be essential for the continuation of your kingdom.
Celebrant: Let this palm be a constant reminder of our own

contradictions, dishonesty and hesitance to help in the
growth of your kingdom;
our unwillingness to give witness to the life you have given
us in your Son, Jesus.
Help us, Lord, now,
We ask you to bless these palms
as signs of contradiction,
signifying not only victory, but martyrdom.
We ask this in the name of Jesus Christ your Son,
who with you and the Spirit, lives forever and ever.

THE GOSPEL:
Matthew 26:1–9.

GOSPEL ACCLAMATION AND PROCESSIONAL:
(All process into church.) "The King of Glory Comes,"
Hymnal for Young Christians, p. 60.
(To be sung upon arrival in church) "All Glory, Praise, and
Honor," *People's Mass Book*, #29.

THE READING OF THE PASSION:
Mark 14:32–72; 15:1–46.

PERIOD OF REFLECTION:
Intermission

PROCESSIONAL:
"O Sacred Head, Surrounded," *People's Mass Book*, #27.

PRAYER OF BLESSING OVER GIFTS:
Only the "Let us pray that my sacrifice and yours . . ."
with its response is used today.

THE TABLE PRAYER

PREFACE:
"De Virtute Crucis," *Missale Romanum Ex Decreto Sacrosancti*

Oecumenici Concilii Vaticani II Instauratum Auctoritate Pauli PP VI Promulgatum, translated by Rev. James D. White:
Father, all-powerful and ever-living God,
 we do well always and everywhere to give you thanks.
Through the life-giving passion of your Son
 the whole world has learned to acknowledge your glory.
With power from the cross beyond all telling
 Christ receives his authority,
 and judgment shines forth upon us all.
And so with the angels and saints,
 we, too, acknowledge your glory and joyfully proclaim:

HYMN OF PRAISE:
 "Praise to the Lord," first verse, *People's Mass Book*, #175.

ACCLAMATION AT CONSECRATION:
 #235a, *People's Mass Book*.

ENDING ACCLAMATION:
 "Praise to the Lord," cited above, third verse.

THE SERVICE OF COMMUNION

THE "OUR FATHER"

RITE OF PEACE

FRACTION RITE:
 Litany of the "Lamb of God"

SONG:
 "Yes, I Shall Arise," *People's Mass Book*, #174.

PERIOD OF REFLECTION:
 Intermission

THE DISMISSAL RITE

PRAYER OF BENEDICTION:
"Lord God, you sent your Son into the world," *Your Word Is Near*, p. 59.

BLESSING AND DISMISSAL

ANNOUNCEMENTS

RECESSIONAL:
"Sion, Sing," *People's Mass Book*, #165.

HOLY THURSDAY II

Theme: A Passover Celebration at the Table of the Lord's Supper

(The Passover Rite may be adapted from any now available, following the general directions given below. Because the entire emphasis is on the Table and the Lord's Supper, the whole service is carried out around the altar-table.)

LIGHTING OF CANDLES:
A woman of the parish, entering from the sacristy, lights the candles. Standing at the altar she prays the prayer beginning, "Blessed are you, Lord, our God, King of the Universe, who has sanctified us by your commandments. . . ."

FIRST READING:
The woman takes her place in the congregation; a reader coming to the altar from the sanctuary reads Luke 22:7–13.

PROCESSIONAL:
"They'll Know We Are Christians by Our Love," *Hymnal for Young Christians*, p. 132.

PRAYER:
The celebrant reads the prayer, "Blessed are you, Lord God, King of the Universe, who has chosen us above all peoples. . . ."

Three Questions:
Three different children ask these questions, respectively:
Why is this night different from all other nights?
What is the meaning of "Pasch"?
What is the meaning of the unleavened bread?
(The celebrant reads the answers to these questions from the Passover Rite, then continues below.)

Celebrant:
It was in this way, and by the blood of the lamb, that the first covenant between God and man was established. In our own time, that covenant is completed, and another, far more

91

lasting agreement has been made which was sealed by the
Blood of the New Lamb, the Blood of the Lamb of God, Jesus
Christ. Preparing that covenant, he lived and walked among
us; it was about this event that the Gospels were written.

THE GOSPEL:
John 13:1–15.

PRAYER OF BLESSING OVER GIFTS:
*(Because gifts are already prepared, the celebrant begins
directly with the Table Prayer.)*

THE TABLE PRAYER

PREFACE:
Blessed are you Lord God, King of the Universe,
    who turns our bread of affliction into bread of life
    and gives us the cup of festivity
    to take us from anguish to joy,
    from darkness to your great light.
Let us therefore sing before the Lord a new hymn:
(Adapted from Passover rite.)

HYMN OF PRAISE:
"Where Charity and Love Prevail," *People's Mass Book*, #121.

ACCLAMATION AT CONSECRATION:
(Spoken) "Whenever we eat this bread . . ." from *The
English-Latin Sacramentary.*

ENDING ACCLAMATION:
"You Alone Are Holy," *Biblical Hymns and Psalms*, Vol. II,
p. 52.

THE SERVICE OF COMMUNION

THE "OUR FATHER"

RITE OF PEACE
After the greeting of peace, all read this prayer together:

"We break bread together for ourselves . . ." in *Eucharistic Liturgies*, p. 41. Begin second sentence with "*We* come."

FRACTION RITE:
Litany of the "Lamb of God"

SONG:
"Whatsoever You Do," *People's Mass Book*, #208.

PERIOD OF REFLECTION:
Intermission
Reading for Meditation (*printed on program*): John 6:53–58. (*During this time preparations are made for procession to repository.*)

PROCESSIONAL:
"Peace, My Friends," *Hymnal for Young Christians*, Vol. II, p. 34.

STRIPPING OF THE ALTAR:
Psalm 22.

GOOD FRIDAY II

Theme: The Passion and Death of Jesus

All of this liturgy is taken from *The English-Latin Sacramentary*
except the following:
Introductory Reading: John 12:24-28.
Prayer:
Lord God, we recall the broken body of Jesus, our brother.
In the broken bread, we remember your promise
    to be the forgiveness of sins.
In the passion of your Christ, our Lord,
    you have conquered death,
    and re-membered the scattered people of your flock.
It is at this table
    that we are remembered and become one in your peace.
We offer this prayer in the name
    of your Son, Jesus Christ, who lives forever and ever.

(The Reading of the Passion follows immediately.)

Music: "O Sacred Head Surrounded," *People's Mass Book*,
    #27, is sung while the celebrant goes to the altar of repose
    for the consecrated bread and wine. "My Shepherd Is the
    Lord" (Ps. 22, Antiphon I), *Twenty-Four Psalms and a
    Canticle*, p. 10, is sung during Communion.

EASTER VIGIL II

Theme: "He Has Risen and Gone before You into Galilee"

THE SERVICE OF THE WORD

PROCESSIONAL:
"Yes, I Shall Arise," *People's Mass Book*, #174.

FIRST READING:
Genesis 1:1–31. May be shortened by omitting repetitious lines and transitions such as, "Evening came and morning came; the fifth day."

RESPONSE:
God, Lord of the Universe,
  you wonderfully created everything that lives
  and more wonderfully by the fire of your care
  have redeemed the works of your hand.
Let our world have the blessing and the fire of your life—
  our world of feelings, of flesh and bone,
  of light and stone and steel,
  a world full of news and people.
Give us our lives with all their cares and pleasures
  but lives enlightened and burning with your presence,
  so that darkness may not surround us,
  but only Jesus Christ, the light of our life,
  who lives with you and with us, forever and ever.

SONG:
"O God, Our Help In Ages Past," third, fourth, and fifth verses, *People's Mass Book*, #185.

SECOND READING:
But man forgot and dimmed the light of creation. Some say he forgot to avoid the fruit of a certain tree; others say he

forgot that he was not a god himself. Still others say that man
forgot that God said creation was good and that man
should rule the earth, not that the earth should rule man.
As man multiplied and filled the earth, so did his forgetfulness,
which became his shame. The wickedness of man's forgetting
covered the earth and spoiled it. So ruined was the creation
that the image of God was hardly discernible; and as the
image faded, so did the Spirit of God. There was, however,
one man who had not forgotten his God—his name was Noah.
Noah's presence was a reminder to God, for Noah was good;
so God remembered his creation and, in remembering,
determined to make it new—to wash it clean, to make it
fertile again so that it would bring forth life, not death.
Through Noah's faithful help, God was made mindful of the
fragments of his good creation and decided to wash from
the face of the earth all that divided it, all that spoiled it. So
it rained—a rain which brought death to death and restored
life. God remembered; and it was good.

RESPONSE:
    Faithful Father, everlasting God,
        we speak and respeak your praises;
        for though we have tasted sin and death in Adam,
        you have never stopped trying to show
        that you are in love with us.
    In the very beginning your Spirit hovered over the waters,
        and then penetrated them
        so that they would give life and sanctify.
    By the deluge of rain you hinted at the marvelous way
        in which your love-life would become a torrent
        upon the earth.
    In the desert your Spirit quickened the dry bones of Israel,
        so that once more life came from death and ashes,
        and your people rose up to be faithful
        in continuing their pilgrimage back to you.
    And within your people, the Church,
        you have never ceased making love
        by your acts of regeneration in the waters of baptism.
    Even now you rescue us from the darkness of our deeds

and make us light-filled people,
born anew in the way of love.

SONG:

"My Soul Is Thirsting" (Ps. 41, Antiphon I), *Twenty-Four Psalms and a Canticle*, p. 16. Use psalm verses 1, 2, 3, 5, 7.

THE GOSPEL:

John 4:6–15.

GOSPEL ACCLAMATION:

Repeat antiphon from above: "My Soul Is Thirsting."

BLESSING OF WATER:

We acknowledge, Lord,
    that by your unseen power
    you work wonders through signs we can see.
Through the use of water
    you prepared for the revelation of baptism.
When the world was first created,
    your Spirit hovered over the waters
    so that even then the waters might have
    the power to produce life.
You made the great flood an image of rebirth
    so that water might stand
    for an end to sin and a beginning of holiness.
You led the children of Abraham
    through the Red Sea on dry ground,
    to free the people from the slavery of Egypt
    and make them a figure of the people of baptism.
In the water of the Jordan
    your only Son was baptized by John,
    and anointed by the Holy Spirit.
Water and blood came forth from his side
    as he hung upon the cross.
When he had risen, he told his disciples
    to baptize with water:
"You are to go and teach all nations,
    and baptize them in the name

of the Father and of the Son and the Holy Spirit."
Look upon your Church
   and open the font of baptism.
May this water receive the gift of the Spirit
   so that man, who was made in your image,
   may be washed clean from sin
   and be born again in new life
   through the sacrament of water and of the Spirit.
(Celebrant touches water with his right hand.)
Lord, send the power of the Holy Spirit
   into this water,
   so that baptism will be
   a kind of death and burial with Christ
   and a resurrection with him to a new life.
Through Christ our Lord.
(Adapted from Blessing of Water in *The English-Latin Sacramentary.)*

RENEWAL OF VOWS, ADMINISTERING OF BAPTISM:
   The New Baptismal Rite, Chapter Two, *Manual of Celebration*, pp. 13–23.
   (After the Anointing before Baptism, the people welcome those to be baptized by reading the following prayer and Gospel passage.)
   The faith we wish to share with you is not a hidden, secret faith of a buried Christ, but faith in a living Christ—risen from the dead. Therefore, we break from this place, as Christ broke from the tomb, and lead you to new life in the Spirit. The risen Christ, after his resurrection, was always recognized by his believers in the breaking of bread, so now we lead you to him as we share his Body and Blood.
   Gospel passage is from Matthew 28:1–7a.
   (If the service began in the basement of the church or in an adjoining building, the congregation, led by the minister and those to be baptized, now move to the church. The ministers and those to be baptized go to the font; the others gather around or face the font from their pews. The Baptismal Rite continues.)

PERIOD OF REFLECTION:
Intermission

PROCESSIONAL:
"Jesus Christ Is Risen Today," *People's Mass Book*, #30.

PRAYER OF BLESSING OVER GIFTS:
Omitted today. Begin Preface immediately.

THE TABLE PRAYER

PREFACE:
Preface for Easter (I) in *The English-Latin Sacramentary*.

HYMN OF PRAISE:
"Holy, Holy, Holy! Lord God Almighty," *People's Mass Book*, #184.

ACCLAMATION AT CONSECRATION:
"Keep in Mind," *People's Mass Book*, #145.

ENDING ACCLAMATION:
"Amen. Amen. Amen. Alleluia," adapted from #108b, *People's Mass Book*.

THE SERVICE OF COMMUNION

THE "OUR FATHER"

RITE OF PEACE

FRACTION RITE:
Litany of the "Lamb of God"

SONG:
"Priestly People," *People's Mass Book*, #146.

PERIOD OF REFLECTION:
Intermission

THE DISMISSAL RITE

PRAYER OF BENEDICTION:
Eucharistic Liturgies, p. 64.

THE EXULTET:
Sung as indicated in *The English-Latin Sacramentary*. The following explanation may be printed on the program:

This announcement is fittingly cast in the rich style of the imperial courts. In this way were royal births and marriages proclaimed to the people and court. During the fifth century, the liturgy began to cast the most solemn prayers in similar formal wording. We should note that there is great emphasis upon the Easter renewal that the Exultet conveys. The whole of creation—heaven, angels, earth, the Church, all peoples, especially all who are present—are invited to join in the celebration because we sing of the glory of the victorious Lord who drives away all darkness.

BLESSING AND DISMISSAL
Blessing as in *Eucharistic Liturgies*, p. 65.

ANNOUNCEMENTS

RECESSIONAL:
"Rejoice, the Lord Is King," *Hymnal for Young Christians*, p. 115.

EASTER SUNDAY II

Theme: The Resurrection of Our Lord, Jesus Christ

THE ENTRANCE RITE

INVITATION TO WORSHIP:
We invite you to share with us in our great joy as we celebrate
the resurrection of our Lord, Jesus Christ. By his resurrection
we know that our faith is not in vain and so we look eagerly
toward our present and future, filled with the hope that
the Lord Jesus is still with us. As all nature begins to rouse
itself from the sluggishness of winter and the appearances of
death, so also, man lifts himself up, once again, by faith in
the Lord. Man comes to a new realization of himself, shorn
as he is by the rigors of Lent. Man steps forward now, the
new creature. Man celebrates on this day all that he can be
by reason of the life, death and resurrection of Jesus Christ.

PROCESSIONAL:
"Jesus Christ Is Risen Today," *People's Mass Book*, #30.

GREETING:
Eucharistic Liturgies, p. 66.

PRAYER OF INVOCATION:
Eucharistic Liturgies, p. 66.

THE SERVICE OF THE WORD

FIRST READING:
Revelation 21:1–4.

GOSPEL ACCLAMATION:
"Alleluia! The Strife Is O'er," first verse, *People's Mass Book*,
#34.

THE GOSPEL:
Luke 24:13–35.

101

GOSPEL ACCLAMATION:
"Alleluia! The Strife Is O'er," cited above, second verse.

HOMILY

PROFESSION OF FAITH:
The Apostles' Creed

GENERAL INTENTIONS:
(*Response:* Risen Savior, hear our prayer.)
Selection from pp. 85–87, *Your Word Is Near.*

PERIOD OF REFLECTION:
Intermission

PROCESSIONAL:
"Alleluia, Sing to Jesus," *The Hymnal of the Protestant
Episcopal Church in the United States of America,* #347.

PRAYER OF BLESSING OVER GIFTS:
Only the "Let us pray that my sacrifice and yours . . ." and
its response is used today.

THE TABLE PRAYER

PREFACE:
First seven lines of "Canon of Death and Resurrection," *The
Experimental Liturgy Book,* p. 69. Conclude with the
following: Together with all those in heaven and those here
on earth, we sing to you now, in praise of your holy name:

HYMN OF PRAISE:
"Praise God, From Whom All Blessings Flow," *People's Mass
Book,* #45.

ACCLAMATION AT CONSECRATION:
"Keep in Mind," *People's Mass Book,* #145.

ENDING ACCLAMATION:
"Amen. Amen. Amen. Alleluia," adapted from #108b, *People's
Mass Book.*

THE SERVICE OF COMMUNION

THE "OUR FATHER"

RITE OF PEACE

FRACTION RITE:
Litany of the "Lamb of God"

SONG:
"At the Lamb's High Feast," *Our Parish Prays and Sings,* #2.

PERIOD OF REFLECTION:
Intermission

THE DISMISSAL RITE

PRAYER OF BENEDICTION:
Eucharistic Liturgies, p. 67.

BLESSING AND DISMISSAL

ANNOUNCEMENTS

RECESSIONAL:
"Christ the Lord Is Risen Today," *People's Mass Book,* #31.

SECOND SUNDAY OF EASTER II

Theme: Mission of a Spirit-Filled People

THE ENTRANCE RITE

INVITATION TO WORSHIP:
The risen Lord gave his Spirit to the apostles. It was a Spirit
which brought them peace, love, and joy. Under the impulse
of that Spirit, the apostolic Church began its mission. We have
celebrated our faith on Easter, increasing our membership
through the waters of holy baptism; today we seek to find
direction and expression of that faith. Since as a Spirit-filled
people we are restless and conscious of the opposites in our
lives and our constant need to resolve and reconcile, we
turn again to the Word of God, the Word made flesh.

PROCESSIONAL:
"At the Lamb's High Feast," *Our Parish Prays and Sings*, #2.

GREETING:
Blessings to you, men and women of faith,
   who come here in peace and in turmoil
   to proclaim the resurrection and to find
   some share in the new life of God's Son.
May the joy and peace of the risen Christ be with you.

PRAYER OF INVOCATION:
"We worship and admire you, God," *Your Word Is Near*,
p. 91. Introduce with:
Remembering that God has done the impossible by raising
   a dead Christ to life, we pray that he will do the same
   for us:

THE SERVICE OF THE WORD

FIRST READING:
Acts 5:12–16.

GOSPEL ACCLAMATION:
"Alleluia, The Strife Is O'er," *People's Mass Book,* #34.

THE GOSPEL:
John 20:19–31.

GOSPEL ACCLAMATION:
"Alleluia, The Strife Is O'er," cited above, third verse.

HOMILY

PROFESSION OF FAITH:
We believe that we,
 members of the Body of Christ, the Church of Jesus Christ,
 are sent to all nations to proclaim the Gospel.
We believe that we must be
 the salt of the earth and light of the world,
 summoned with special grace
 to save and renew every creature.
We believe that we are a pilgrim and missionary Church
 by nature
 and we further affirm that in order to establish
 peace and communion between sinful human beings and
  God,
 as well as to fashion men into a fraternal community,
 God sent his only Son, clothed in our flesh,
 that he might reconcile the world to himself.
We believe that we who live by his Spirit
 and are annointed in his grace
 are also sent to bring good news to the poor,
 to heal the brokenhearted and to proclaim
 rescue to the captives and sight to the blind.
We firmly believe that the mission of the Church,
 and therefore our mission, is fulfilled
 by activity which makes us present to all men,
 so that wherever we live,
 we are bound to show forth
 by the example of our lives and by our speech,

the new man we have put on at baptism,
and the power of the Holy Spirit we have from confirmation.
Prompted by that Spirit,
    we walk the road Christ walked—
    a road of poverty, obedience, of service and
    self-sacrifice—
    so that others who see our good works
    will perceive the real meaning of human life
    and glorify the Father forever.
Amen.
(Based on the Preface and Chapter I of the "Decree on the
Missionary Activity of the Church" of Vatican II.)

GENERAL INTENTIONS:
    (*Response:* Risen Savior, hear our prayer.)
    Selection from pp. 85–87, *Your Word Is Near.*

PERIOD OF REFLECTION:
    Intermission

PROCESSIONAL:
    "Christ the Lord Is Risen Today," *People's Mass Book,* #31.

PRAYER OF BLESSING OVER GIFTS:
    Only the "Let us pray that my sacrifice and yours . . ." and
    its response is used today.

THE TABLE PRAYER

PREFACE:
    Father, we speak of the wonders you perform;
        we praise you for raising to life your Son and our
        brother, Jesus.
    He has become the new Adam,
        born of the earth, broken at the hands of men;
        yet, as the grain of wheat dying to bring
        a rich harvest,

he has disarmed death and mourning and suffering,
   so that their sting does not last forever.
He has become the song on every tongue,
   the Word shared among us,
   the Word we shall go on speaking and meeting all of
   our lives
   so that your faithfulness toward us will be known
   among our children forever.
With all of creation straining to burst the bonds of death
   and with all of your faithful rising from their old selves,
   we praise you, singing together:

HYMN OF PRAISE:
   "Holy, Holy, Holy! Lord God Almighty," *People's Mass Book*,
   #184.

ACCLAMATION AT CONSECRATION:
   #235a, *People's Mass Book*.

ENDING ACCLAMATION:
   "Keep in Mind," *People's Mass Book*, #145.

THE SERVICE OF COMMUNION

THE "OUR FATHER"

RITE OF PEACE

FRACTION RITE:
   Litany of the "Lamb of God"

SONG:
   "O Sons and Daughters," *People's Mass Book*, #32.

PERIOD OF REFLECTION:
   Intermission

THE DISMISSAL RITE

PRAYER OF BENEDICTION:

Lord God, your lavish faithfulness puts us to shame.
You have never given up on us, even though our history
    is one of unfaithfulness and discouragement.
You have raised the dead to life in your Son,
    and are raising us to new life
    each time we set aside ourselves for someone else.
Having broken bread and shared
    the Body and Blood—the New Life of Jesus,
    we praise you and bless your name for your
    faithfulness and mercy.
In Jesus' name we pray forever and ever.

BLESSING AND DISMISSAL

ANNOUNCEMENTS

RECESSIONAL:

"A Mighty Fortress Is Our God," *People's Mass Book*, #187.

THIRD SUNDAY OF EASTER II

Theme: The Difficulties of Discipleship

THE ENTRANCE RITE

INVITATION TO WORSHIP:
Last Sunday's liturgy brought to our attention the faith we
celebrate at Easter time, and the mission of the believing
community, prompted by that faith, to lead the way to a
new creation. All of us—our new fellow Christians, you and I
—today gather to celebrate, give thanks and renew our own
beginnings in faith. In the liturgy of the Word today we will
hear of the apostles' difficulty with their new Easter faith;
and in the Gospel we will recall the risen Lord's invitation
to be active people, alive with faith and with courage, as a
people anointed and consecrated through baptism and
confirmation.

PROCESSIONAL:
"At the Lamb's High Feast," *Our Parish Prays and Sings*, #2.

GREETING:
Blessings and courage to you who have come
   in acceptance of the Lord's invitation to follow him.
May the strength and the peace of the risen Christ
   be with you.

PRAYER OF INVOCATION:
Aware of the mission of God's people, and of our need for
   his presence to give us direction and renewal, let us pray:
Father, the way of your Son is already too clear for us,
   and we are intimidated at the thought
   of following him through betrayal by friends,
   a dark night of loneliness, and the cross,
   in order to emerge victorious.
Yet we come here again to hear your words of invitation.
Strengthened by the risen, living Body and Blood of your Son,

we too will be victorious—
all to your honor and glory forever and ever.

THE SERVICE OF THE WORD

FIRST READING:
Acts 5:27–42.

RESPONSE:
"A Prayer of Discipleship," *Discovery in Prayer,* p. 105. Omit
the three sentences in parentheses for oral reading.

SECOND READING:
Omitted today.

GOSPEL ACCLAMATION:
"Alleluia, The Strife Is O'er," first verse, *People's Mass Book,*
#34.

THE GOSPEL:
John 21:1–19.

GOSPEL ACCLAMATION:
"Alleluia, The Strife Is O'er," cited above, second verse.

HOMILY

PROFESSION OF FAITH:
"Mission" Creed as in liturgy for preceding Sunday.

GENERAL INTENTIONS:
(*Response:* Risen Savior, hear our prayer.)
Selection from pp. 98–99, *Your Word Is Near.*

PERIOD OF REFLECTION:
Intermission

PROCESSIONAL:
"Sion Sing," *People's Mass Book,* #165.

PRAYER OF BLESSING OVER GIFTS:
Only the "Let us pray that my sacrifice and yours . . ." and
its response is used today.

THE TABLE PRAYER

PREFACE:
"De Vita Nova in Christo," *Missale Romanum Ex Decreto
Sacrosancti Oecumenici Concilii Vaticani II Instauratum
Auctoritate Pauli PP VI Promulgatum,* translated by Rev.
James D. White:
Father, all-powerful and ever-living God,
   we do well always and everywhere to give you thanks
   and praise through Jesus Christ our Lord.
We praise you with greater joy than ever
   in this Easter season
   when Christ becomes our paschal sacrifice.
Through him the sons of light have risen to eternal life
   and the gates of heaven have opened to the faithful.
By his death we are saved from death
   and in his resurrection the life of every man is renewed.
And so it is that, overflowing with Easter joy,
   the earth and every creature raise their voices,
   as together with all the power of heaven
   they endlessly proclaim:

HYMN OF PRAISE:
"Praise to the Lord," first verse, *People's Mass Book,* #175.

ACCLAMATION AT CONSECRATION:
#190b, *People's Mass Book.*

ENDING ACCLAMATION:
"Praise to the Lord," cited above, third verse.

THE SERVICE OF COMMUNION

THE "OUR FATHER"

RITE OF PEACE

FRACTION RITE:
Litany of the "Lamb of God"

SONG:
"Priestly People," *People's Mass Book*, #146.

PERIOD OF REFLECTION:
Intermission
Reading for Meditation (*printed on program*): "I think I
am ready . . . ," *Discovery in Prayer*, p. 105.

THE DISMISSAL RITE

PRAYER OF BENEDICTION:
We have broken bread—
    shared the risen, living Body of Jesus Christ.
Like this bread, Father, we are to be broken,
    that from the fragments of broken habits,
    broken attitudes, and a broken past,
    we may rise to be your new people,
    giving you fitting praise and glory
    in all that we do and say today and every day to come,
    forever and ever.

BLESSING AND DISMISSAL

ANNOUNCEMENTS

RECESSIONAL:
"A Mighty Fortress Is Our God," *People's Mass Book*, #187.

FOURTH SUNDAY OF EASTER II

Theme: A Celebration in Praise of Christ, The Good Shepherd

THE ENTRANCE RITE

INVITATION TO WORSHIP:
Today we hear from the author of the letter to the Hebrews
that Jesus is our high priest—a man taken from among men,
who can sympathize with those who are ignorant and
uncertain because he too lives within the limitations of
weakness. We gather to remember that Jesus is our only
Priest; those who are appointed and called to express his
priesthood in flesh and blood today are called simply to be
his spokesman, preaching not themselves, but Christ, the
Word of God for every man.

PROCESSIONAL:
"Alleluia, Sing to Jesus," *The Hymnal of the Protestant
Episcopal Church in the United States of America*, #347.

GREETING:
Wisdom and understanding be yours
    from Jesus Christ our High Priest
    who comes among us to serve and not be served,
    to bring us light and lead us from darkness.

PRAYER OF INVOCATION:
Mindful that Jesus is our Priest and that the Church is called
to be the visible sign of his priesthood in the world, let us pray:
Eternal Father, you have given your Son to us.
He was a man and, like us, mortal.
He lived without power in this world.
You gave him the right to speak—he is your Word—
    but he could not find a hearing.
We pray that we who are called to serve and not be served
    may, in our sinfulness, always hold onto him
    and grow in a deeper understanding of the service

113

to which we are called.
May we handle with great care the Word of your Son,
    which we carry in the frailty of our person.
We ask this through Jesus your Son
    who with the Spirit lives as God, forever and ever.
(Adapted from p. 58, *Your Word Is Near.*)

THE SERVICE OF THE WORD

FIRST READING:
    Isaiah 42:1–7.

RESPONSE:
    " 'God's word is a living thing!' . . ." through ". . . God
    doesn't speak to," *That Man Is You*, p. 25. Alternate lines
    between reader and people.

SECOND READING:
    Hebrews 5:1–10.

GOSPEL ACCLAMATION:
    "Alleluia! The Strife Is O'er," first verse, *People's Mass Book*,
    #34.

THE GOSPEL:
    Mark 10:42–45.

GOSPEL ACCLAMATION:
    "Alleluia! The Strife Is O'er," cited above, second verse.

HOMILY

PROFESSION OF FAITH:
    Use the first seven lines of "Canon of the Word of God,"
    The Experimental Liturgy Book, p. 84.
    Add the following: We praise you together with your
    life-giving Spirit through Jesus Christ. Amen.

GENERAL INTENTIONS:

(*Response:* Risen Savior, hear our prayer.)

That each man, claiming to be Christian, will listen to the cries of this world, and respond with open heart and mind, we pray to the Lord:

That priests will find peace as they try daily to imitate Jesus in their work of service to people, we pray to the Lord:

For married people who have drifted apart from each other; for priests who have grown tired in preaching the Word of God, we pray to the Lord:

For those crucified with Christ through the sufferings of mankind in this present age; for those overwhelmed by disasters, we pray to the Lord:

That young men and women throughout the Church come to realize that a life given to the "glory of God" is given to help mankind become fully alive, we pray to the Lord.

PERIOD OF REFLECTION:

Intermission

PROCESSIONAL:

"Priestly People," *People's Mass Book,* #146.

PRAYER OF BLESSING OVER GIFTS:

Only the "Let us pray that my sacrifice and yours ..." and its response is used today.

THE TABLE PRAYER

PREFACE:

For life and love, for bread and wine
   in the hands of Jesus,
      we gather to give you thanks, God and Father.
We praise you for what you have done
   to your people whom you wish to be
      your partner in a covenant of love.
By pouring out your Spirit of life,
   you have led us from captivity;

you nourish us with your Word
and consecrate us to be a priestly people.
By your Spirit, you enliven us to carry
your Good News on our shoulders
and your Word in our mouths,
so that these tidings may be borne to anyone,
anywhere in this world.
Once more we await a new beginning from you,
Father and Lord Spirit, through Jesus Christ.
With all of creation and the hosts of heaven,
we praise you, singing together:

HYMN OF PRAISE:
"Praise the Lord of Heaven," *People's Mass Book,* #180.

ACCLAMATION AT CONSECRATION:
#235a, *People's Mass Book.*

ENDING ACCLAMATION:
#108b, *People's Mass Book.*

THE SERVICE OF COMMUNION

THE "OUR FATHER"

RITE OF PEACE

FRACTION RITE:
Litany of the "Lamb of God"

SONG:
"My Shepherd Is the Lord," (Ps. 22, Antiphon I),
Twenty-Four Psalms and a Canticle, p. 10.

PERIOD OF REFLECTION:
Intermission

THE DISMISSAL RITE

PRAYER OF BENEDICTION:

> Lord God, as a miracle of love,
>> as a Word that makes men free,
>> your Son has come to us,
>> and where he comes, life is no longer dark and fearful.
>
> We pray that he, our Priest, may come to life among us here,
>> that we may not be ensnared in confusion,
>> obsessed with suspicion,
>> but that we may be filled with faith, courage, and adventure
>> in discovering our mission in this world.
>
> This we ask through Jesus Christ
>> who lives and gives you glory through us
>> now and forever and ever.
>
> (Adapted from "Lord God, as a miracle of humanity and love," *Your Word Is Near*, p. 60.)

BLESSING AND DISMISSAL

ANNOUNCEMENTS

RECESSIONAL:

> "All Men on Earth," *People's Mass Book*, #36.

FIFTH SUNDAY OF EASTER II

Theme: Motherhood: Sign of Covenant

THE ENTRANCE RITE

INVITATION TO WORSHIP:

In the weeks after Easter we have been considering our
"Easter faith" and what it does to us in terms of our "mission"
to the world. There is perhaps no better example of this
living faith than the example of service and love which is
shown by a mother. But the role of the mother is something
that is not possible without placing it within the larger context
of the initial community, the family, or the primary
relationship of husband and wife. Just as the life and faith of
the Christian are vague and idealistic until they are placed in
the world, so the concept of "mother" is vague and idealistic
when considered alone. But place the notion of mother into
a family, and the role becomes livable, possible and, best
of all, salvific for those who seek to build God's kingdom
on earth by fulfilling this role. So it is with hearts very
conscious of and very grateful to the mothers who are
present in this Eucharistic celebration—present both in the
reality of this moment, and present in the spirit of the risen
Christ—that we begin our celebration in song.

PROCESSIONAL:

"All Men on Earth," *People's Mass Book*, #36.

GREETING:

Wisdom and strength be yours
    from Jesus Christ, the Word of God,
    who speaks to the Father's will,
    who by his life and his words has directed us
    to the Father's kingdom.
May the love and the peace of the risen Lord be with you.

118

PRAYER OF INVOCATION:

Remembering that our mothers, as part of the covenant
of marriage, are signs to us of the covenant between God
and his Church, let us pray:
God, you are intimately bound to all of us
  by your faithful covenant with man.
We ask you to let us experience your faithfulness
  in good times and in bad.
We also pray that we may, in your name,
  find the strength to love and honor
  those you have given us as mothers;
  to help them and remain faithful to them
  all our lives until death for all eternity.
(Adapted from "God, you are intimately bound," *Your Word
Is Near*, p. 110.)

THE SERVICE OF THE WORD

FIRST READING:
Proverbs 31:10–31.

RESPONSE:
1 John 4:15–19.

SECOND READING:
Omitted today.

GOSPEL ACCLAMATION:
"Your Word, O Lord," *Biblical Hymns and Psalms*, Vol. II,
p. 88. This is sung by cantor; people respond with "Alleluia,
Alleluia," as indicated.

THE GOSPEL:
John 4:1–19, 25–30, 39–42.

GOSPEL ACCLAMATION:
"Alleluia, Alleluia," repeated from Gospel Acclamation above.

HOMILY

GENERAL INTENTIONS:
(*Response:* Risen Savior, hear our prayer.)
In loving remembrance of mothers who have died, let us
pray to the Lord:
With gratitude to those who are still with us doing the things
that only a mother can do best, let us pray to the Lord:
For the safe delivery of those now with child, let us pray
to the Lord:
For those mothers who are hurt, disappointed and confused,
let us pray to the Lord:

PERIOD OF REFLECTION:
Intermission

PROCESSIONAL:
"We Gather Together," *People's Mass Book,* #53.

PRAYER OF BLESSING OVER GIFTS:
Only the "Let us pray that my sacrifice and yours . . ." and
its response is used today.

THE TABLE PRAYER

PREFACE:
With joy in our hearts, we gather here, eternal Father,
to share our happiness in gratitude
for all you have done for us and given us.
You created people as man and woman,
knowing it was not good for us to be alone.
By the sacrament of marriage and the role of mother,
you have hinted to us that we are not abandoned.
By this prayer of thanksgiving,
by this breaking of bread
and sharing of your Son's Body and Blood
we renew your covenant between person and person
and create a bond of affection between heart and heart.
Be as close to us as the body of the other

and let us experience that everything you make is good.
Conscious of our oneness with you
   through your Son and all creation,
   we sing this hymn of praise:
(Adapted from "You created people as man and woman,"
Your Word Is Near, p. 109.)

HYMN OF PRAISE:
   "Praise God, From Whom All Blessings Flow," *People's Mass
Book*, #45.

ACCLAMATION AT CONSECRATION:
   #190b, *People's Mass Book*.

ENDING ACCLAMATION:
   #108b, *People's Mass Book*.

THE SERVICE OF COMMUNION

THE "OUR FATHER"

RITE OF PEACE

FRACTION RITE:
   Litany of the "Lamb of God"

SONG:
   "Come and Eat of My Bread" (Antiphon II), *People's Mass
Book*, #172.

PERIOD OF REFLECTION:
   Intermission

THE DISMISSAL RITE

PRAYER OF BENEDICTION:
   God our Father, in your loving kindness
     you have given us the sign of motherhood
     as a reminder of your care for us.

We pray that by this sharing of your Son's Body and Blood,
as man and wife, as friends and neighbors,
we may follow the example of your Son, Jesus Christ—
his example of love and respect for his fellow men,
so that we may, in his spirit, be happy
and believe that you are the source of all love,
that you are love itself, our God and our Father,
you who live with the Son and the Spirit, forever and ever.
(Adapted from "God, it is your work and your promise,"
Your Word Is Near, p. 109.)

BLESSING AND DISMISSAL

ANNOUNCEMENTS

RECESSIONAL:
"Christ the Lord Is Risen Today," *People's Mass Book,* #31.

SIXTH SUNDAY OF EASTER II

Theme: A Celebration of the Church-at-Work among Men

THE ENTRANCE RITE

INVITATION TO WORSHIP:
Today's Eucharistic celebration gives us cause to consider
our Easter faith and the alteration it should be making in
our lives. The apostles and their new Christians were making
difficult adjustments in their lives because of the Christ-event.
There was a significant adjustment when, as the faith spread
to the Gentiles, they began to realize that they were no
longer able to live by Jewish tradition. This difficulty erupted
into a controversy which had to be settled by a council. The
lesson learned by the early Church through that experience
is one we are still in need of learning—catholicity or
universality is the very fundamental mark of the Church.

PROCESSIONAL:
"We Gather Together," *People's Mass Book,* #53.

GREETING:
Wisdom and grace to you who are here in peace
    to hear the Word of God
    and to shape your own lives by his will.
May the courage and the spirit of the risen Christ be with you.

PRAYER OF INVOCATION:
Aware that our faith has been renewed by our Easter
    celebration, we pray:
Almighty Father we bless the power of your Word, Jesus
    Christ.
In him we have become a new people,
    able to overcome anything, even death,
    if it becomes an obstacle to our growth in love.
As the apostles and their faithful
    resolved their differences in peace,
    help us to do the same,

123

as we grow ever stronger in our faith.
We offer this prayer and all our lives to you
through Jesus your Son, who with the Spirit,
lives and reigns forever and ever.

THE SERVICE OF THE WORD

FIRST READING:
Acts 15:1–2, 22–31.

RESPONSE:
James 1:22–25.

SECOND READING:
Revelation 21:10–14, 22–23.

GOSPEL ACCLAMATION:
"Your Word, O Lord," *Biblical Hymns and Psalms*, Vol. II,
p. 88. This is sung by cantor; people respond with "Alleluia,
Alleluia," as indicated.

THE GOSPEL:
John 14:23–29.

GOSPEL ACCLAMATION:
"Alleluia, Alleluia," repeated from Gospel Acclamation above.

HOMILY

GENERAL INTENTIONS:
(*Response:* Risen Savior, hear our prayer.)
Selection from pp. 112–113, *Your Word Is Near.*

PERIOD OF REFLECTION:
Intermission

PROCESSIONAL:
"Priestly People," *People's Mass Book,* #146.

PRAYER OF BLESSING OVER GIFTS:
Only the "Let us pray that my sacrifice and yours . . ." and
its response is used today.

THE TABLE PRAYER

PREFACE:
"Eucharistic Prayer of Human Unity," *The Experimental
Liturgy Book*, p. 100. Insert between first and second
sentences: We praise you especially at this season of Easter
when Christ has become our joy and our hope.

HYMN OF PRAISE:
"Holy, Holy, Holy! Lord God Almighty," *People's Mass Book*,
#184.

ACCLAMATION AT CONSECRATION:
#190b, *People's Mass Book*.

ENDING ACCLAMATION:
#108b, *People's Mass Book*.

THE SERVICE OF COMMUNION

THE "OUR FATHER"

RITE OF PEACE

FRACTION RITE:
Litany of the "Lamb of God"

SONG:
"Come and Eat of My Bread" (Antiphon II), *People's Mass
Book*, #172.

PERIOD OF REFLECTION:
Intermission

THE DISMISSAL RITE

PRAYER OF BENEDICTION:
Lord, Father Almighty, by this action we have sought
  to remember your Son, Jesus Christ, your Word,
  dismembered and forgotten so often
  by our private acts of selfishness.
We have brought him again to life,
  taken part in the action of resurrection,
  as by this communion we have become his Body—
  your sons and daughters.
May we give you fitting praise and service
  today and in the days to come, forever and ever.

BLESSING AND DISMISSAL

ANNOUNCEMENTS

RECESSIONAL:
"They'll Know We Are Christians by Our Love," *Hymnal
for Young Christians*, p. 132.

FESTIVAL OF THE ASCENSION II

Theme: Ascension/Penetration

THE ENTRANCE RITE

INVITATION TO WORSHIP:
Forty days after the resurrection Jesus finally left his disciples
or, rather, changed the way he was present with them. Since
Easter he had appeared to them a number of times, eaten
with them, and talked with them. They knew he had been
raised to life. Before leaving, however, he asked them to
wait in Jerusalem for the Holy Spirit, who would equip
and graduate them to be witnesses for him throughout the
world. And he promised to come again. Today we remember
that while Jesus disappeared, he did not leave us. We
remember that he is with us to energize all of creation so
that we ascend and return to the Father. The celebration of
Jesus' ascension is less the poetic image of him soaring
upward, glistening like some huge diamond in the sky, than
it is his penetration into those who believe in him. To
celebrate this festival is to remember that the light which is
Christ is put into us to continue his transformation of the
world.

PROCESSIONAL:
"The Church's One Foundation," Samuel Wesley, *People's
Mass Book,* #223.

GREETING:
Praise be to the Father of our Lord Jesus Christ
in whom he has made known to us his purpose:
that all the universe might be brought into a unity
in Christ, risen and ascended.

PRAYER OF INVOCATION:
Eucharistic Liturgies, p. 78. Omit the first sentence. Introduce
second sentence thus: Father, because of his total self-giving
to you and to our world, you welcome Jesus into your sight. . . ."

THE SERVICE OF THE WORD

FIRST READING:
  "I Would Like to Rise Very High," *Prayers,* pp. 13–15, up to
  concluding stanza (five lines) which is used as response.

RESPONSE:
  Last five lines of work cited directly above. Add the
  following: For having the eyes of my heart enlightened, I
  come to know the hope and transformation to which I am
  called.

SECOND READING:
  Acts 1:3–11.

GOSPEL ACCLAMATION:
  "Let the Earth Rejoice and Sing," first verse, *People's Mass
  Book,* #39.

THE GOSPEL:
  Luke 24:46–53.

GOSPEL ACCLAMATION:
  "Let the Earth Rejoice and Sing," cited above, second verse.

HOMILY

GENERAL INTENTIONS:
  (*Response:* Lord Jesus, send us your Spirit.)
  Selection from p. 99 and p. 147, *Your Word Is Near.*

EXTINGUISHING THE PASCHAL CANDLE:
  (*After the celebrant reminds the people of the significance
  of the Paschal Candle, it is extinguished as all pray together
  the following:*)
  We give you thanks, O Lord, because you have enlightened us
    by revealing incorruptible light.
  Having lived in this Easter light,
    and come to the beginning of our journey to you,
    we know that we are not left on our own.

You make your dwelling among us—we cling to this grace.
Happy with the light of day you created for us
 and not lacking a light for our nights,
 we glorify you through Jesus,
 who today ascends to you and yet who is with us,
 making us wise and strong to build your city on earth.
 (Adapted from Hippolytus.)

PERIOD OF REFLECTION:
 Intermission

PROCESSIONAL:
 "Praise the Lord of Heaven," *People's Mass Book,* #180.

PRAYER OF BLESSING OVER GIFTS:
 Only the "Let us pray that my sacrifice and yours . . ." and
 its response is used today.

THE TABLE PRAYER

PREFACE:
 "Canon of the Sons of God," *Eucharistic Liturgies,* p. 194.
 Substitute the following for the last sentence: Because you
 have given us the light of Christ, making us signs of your
 brilliant life and love, we find the courage to stand and sing:

HYMN OF PRAISE:
 "All Men on Earth," *People's Mass Book,* #36.

ACCLAMATION AT CONSECRATION:
 #235a, *People's Mass Book.*

ENDING ACCLAMATION:
 "Praise to the Lord," *People's Mass Book,* #175.

THE SERVICE OF COMMUNION

THE "OUR FATHER"

RITE OF PEACE

FRACTION RITE:
Litany of the "Lamb of God"

SONG:
"We Shall Go Up with Joy" (Ps. 121, Antiphon I),
Twenty-Four Psalms and a Canticle, p. 42.

PERIOD OF REFLECTION:
Intermission

THE DISMISSAL RITE

PRAYER OF BENEDICTION:
Father, we have been sent into the world
   to speak your good news to men.
We will not stand by idle,
   for our life is now
   and there is much for us to do.
Bless us with your Spirit—
The Spirit who gives us courage to go on,
The Spirit who makes us honest,
The Spirit who teaches us how to love.
We await your strengthening Spirit,
   for only then will we be honest witnesses to your Son.
Through him may we give you praise
   now and in all days to come
   forever and ever.
(Adapted from *Eucharistic Liturgies*, p. 79.)

BLESSING AND DISMISSAL

ANNOUNCEMENTS

RECESSIONAL:
"A Mighty Fortress Is Our God," *People's Mass Book*, #187.

SUNDAY AFTER ASCENSION II

Theme: A People Formed by the Spirit

THE ENTRANCE RITE

INVITATION TO WORSHIP:
Vatican Council II in *Horizons of Hope,* p. 78.

PROCESSIONAL:
"We Gather Together," *People's Mass Book,* #53.

GREETING:
Eucharistic Liturgies, p. 80.

PRAYER OF INVOCATION:
Eucharistic Liturgies, p. 80. Omit third, fourth, and fifth sentences.

THE SERVICE OF THE WORD

FIRST READING:
1 Peter 4:1–11.

RESPONSE:
"How many times, God," *Your Word Is Near,* p. 19.

SECOND READING:
Omitted today.

GOSPEL ACCLAMATION:
"Alleluia, Alleluia," *Biblical Hymns and Psalms,* p. 86.

THE GOSPEL:
John 15:18–27.

GOSPEL ACCLAMATION:
Repeat from above.

HOMILY

GENERAL INTENTIONS:
(*Response:* Lord Jesus, send us your Spirit.)
Selection from pp. 126–127, *Your Word Is Near.*

PERIOD OF REFLECTION:
Intermission

PROCESSIONAL:
"Priestly People," *People's Mass Book,* #146.

PRAYER OF BLESSING OVER GIFTS:
Only the "Let us pray that my sacrifice and yours . . ." and
its response is used today.

THE TABLE PRAYER

PREFACE:
"Canon of the Sons of God," *Eucharistic Liturgies,* p. 194.
Substitute the following for the last sentence: Because you
have given us the light of Christ, making us signs of your
brilliant life and love, we find the courage to stand and sing:

HYMN OF PRAISE:
"Praise to the Lord," *People's Mass Book,* #175.

ACCLAMATION AT CONSECRATION:
"Keep in Mind," *People's Mass Book,* #145.

ENDING ACCLAMATION:
#108b, *People's Mass Book.*

THE SERVICE OF COMMUNION

THE "OUR FATHER"

RITE OF PEACE

FRACTION RITE:
Litany of the "Lamb of God"

SONG:
"Peace, My Friends," *Hymnal for Young Christians*, Vol. II, p. 34.

PERIOD OF REFLECTION:
Intermission

THE DISMISSAL RITE

PRAYER OF BENEDICTION:
Eucharistic Liturgies, p. 81.

BLESSING AND DISMISSAL

ANNOUNCEMENTS

RECESSIONAL:
"They'll Know We Are Christians," *Hymnal for Young Christians*, p. 132.

PENTECOST SUNDAY II

Theme: A People Made One in the Spirit

THE ENTRANCE RITE

INVITATION TO WORSHIP:
Ten days ago we celebrated the ascension of our Lord into heaven. As the Easter candle was extinguished, we experienced a sense of loss, a touch of sadness, as surely the apostles must have as they realized that Christ's visible presence was not meant to continue. On this occasion Jesus told the apostles: "Go into the whole world and proclaim the good news to the whole of creation." He prepared the apostles to know and accept the Holy Spirit; they were not to be left abandoned and helpless. "You shall receive power when the Holy Spirit comes upon you, and you shall be witnesses for me in Jerusalem and in Judea, and in Samaria, and even to the very ends of the earth." The Holy Spirit, who calls all men to Christ by the preaching of the Gospel, stirs up in their hearts the obedience of faith. Our hearts embrace also those brothers and communities not yet living with us in full communion. To them we are linked by our profession of the Father, and the Son, and the Holy Spirit, and by the bond of charity. Under the powerful impulse of the Holy Spirit, we advance toward truth, love, unity and peace.

PROCESSIONAL:
"O God, Almighty Father," *Our Parish Prays and Sings,* #12.

GREETING:
The Spirit of the Lord is upon us,
fully confirming us in the mission
of preaching the good news to every creature.

PRAYER OF INVOCATION:
With hearts grateful for the indwelling of the Spirit,
let us pray:

134

Father, we thank you for the gift of your Spirit
  who makes us mindful of our desires
  to search for truth and love.
May we always show to you fitting praise and thanks
  by each becoming a sign and cause
  of unity within the family of your people.
Let our day be a new Pentecost,
  that we accept the promise of your Son,
  that you would give us a new heart,
  and put a new spirit within us.
All glory be to you, Father, and to your Son,
  and to your Holy Spirit, now and forever.
(Adapted from *Eucharistic Liturgies*, p. 82.)

THE SERVICE OF THE WORD

FIRST READING:
  Acts 2:1-11.

RESPONSE:
Reader: When the work which the Father had given the Son to
  do on earth was accomplished, the Holy Spirit was sent on
  the day of Pentecost. Let us prayerfully read together from
  the Documents of Vatican II, as found on your program.
People: All believers would have access to the Father through
  Christ in the one Spirit. The Spirit dwells in the Church and
  in the hearts of the faithful. The Spirit guides the Church
  into the fullness of truth, and gives her unity of fellowship
  and service. We are a people made one with the unity of the
  Father, the Son, and the Holy Spirit.
  (Adaptation of Paragraph 4, Chapter I, *The Constitution on
  the Church of Vatican Council II*.)

SECOND READING:
  1 Corinthians 12:3a-7, 12-13.

GOSPEL ACCLAMATION:
  (*Spoken*) Alleluia. Come, Holy Spirit, fill the hearts of your
  faithful; and kindle in them the fire of your love. Alleluia.

THE GOSPEL:
   John 20:19–23.

HOMILY

PROFESSION OF FAITH:
   "Mission Creed" as in liturgy for Second Sunday of Easter II.

GENERAL INTENTIONS:
   (*Response:* Lord, hear our prayer, and fill us with your
   Spirit.)
   That the Holy Spirit will guide the Church in all
      her teachings, we pray to the Lord:
   That the people of the pilgrim Church will respond to the
      loving truths given them through the teaching of the Holy
      Spirit, we pray to the Lord:
   That we may listen to each other as the Spirit works in
      each individual, we pray to the Lord:
   That we be willing to accept guidance and suggestions
      given to us by those placed in authority by the Father,
      the Son and the Holy Spirit, we pray to the Lord:
   For newly ordained priests, in thanksgiving for their lives
      as they come to serve us in Christ's name, we pray to the
      Lord:

PERIOD OF REFLECTION:
   Intermission

PROCESSIONAL:
   "Send Forth Your Spirit" (Ps. 104), *Biblical Hymns and
   Psalms,* p. 34.

PRAYER OF BLESSING OVER GIFTS:
   Only the "Let us pray that my sacrifice and yours . . ." and
   its response is used today.

THE TABLE PRAYER

PREFACE:
   Preface for Pentecost, *The English-Latin Sacramentary.*

HYMN OF PRAISE:
"Praise God, From Whom All Blessings Flow," *People's Mass Book*, #45.

ACCLAMATION AT CONSECRATION:
#235a, *People's Mass Book.*

ENDING ACCLAMATION:
#108b, *People's Mass Book.*

THE SERVICE OF COMMUNION

THE "OUR FATHER"

RITE OF PEACE

FRACTION RITE:
Litany of the "Lamb of God"

SONG:
"Grant to Us" (Jer. 31:31–34), *Biblical Hymns and Psalms*, p. 40.

PERIOD OF REFLECTION:
Intermission

THE DISMISSAL RITE

PRAYER OF BENEDICTION:
Father, once when the world was dark and helpless,
   you breathed your Spirit upon it and gave it life.
This same Spirit comes to us now
   with the same promise of life and hope.
May we now fully confirm our mission
   received from your hands,
   and take your message of life
   to all nations and peoples,
   even to the ends of the earth,
   so that in the heart of every man

your name may be praised forever and ever.
(Adapted from *Eucharistic Liturgies,* p. 83.)

BLESSING AND DISMISSAL

ANNOUNCEMENTS

RECESSIONAL:
"Holy, Holy, Holy! Lord God Almighty," *People's Mass Book,*
#184.

TRINITY SUNDAY II

Theme: A Celebration of Human Friendship

THE ENTRANCE RITE

INVITATION TO WORSHIP:
Today, the Christian people are invited to consider the close
and intimate relationship among God the Father, God the
Son, and God the Holy Spirit. This mystery of the Christian
faith escapes our wildest imagination. Indeed, it is only
through the revelation offered to us by Jesus that we are
even exposed to the idea of a Trinity and the various
relationships in God. In an attempt to grasp some
understanding of this mystery and of our relationship with
God, let us consider the warm and very human relationship
which we experience between friend and friend. Let us begin
our celebration by reading together the words of Diane
Plummer as found on your program:
Diane Plummer in *Horizons of Hope*, p. 251.

PROCESSIONAL:
"O God, Almighty Father," *Our Parish Prays and Sings*, #12.

GREETING:
May the love and joy we find in our friendships with others
    bring us to a better grasp of our God
    who lives as Father, Son and Holy Spirit.

PRAYER OF INVOCATION:
Mindful of an ever-present yearning in our hearts for peace
    and satisfaction, let us pray:
O God, you who have revealed yourself to us as a loving
    Father,
    we are a people often confused,
    caught up as we are in the countless and varied
    experiences of life.
We seek a path, a way of thinking and acting
    that can offer us some stability in our ever-changing world.
As we consider the written words of men

and the Word of your Son, Jesus,
we hope to capture some inkling of the Spirit of truth
so that we might take on or continue a life
which brings us to full union with you.
We hope for this, strengthened as we are
by your Son Jesus' Spirit,
they who live with you as God, forever and ever.

THE SERVICE OF THE WORD

FIRST READING:
Rosemary Haughton in *Listen to Love*, p. 203.

RESPONSE:
Ecclesiastes 4:9–12, found in *Listen to Love*, p. 241.

SECOND READING:
Ecclesiasticus 6:5–17.

GOSPEL ACCLAMATION:
"Your Word, O Lord," *Biblical Hymns and Psalms*, Vol. II,
p. 88. This is sung by the cantor; people respond with
"Alleluia, Alleluia," as indicated.

THE GOSPEL:
John 14:5–21, 25–26.

GOSPEL ACCLAMATION:
"Alleluia, Alleluia," repeated from Gospel Acclamation above.

HOMILY

PROFESSION OF FAITH:
Act of Faith, *The Underground Mass Book*, p. 23.

GENERAL INTENTIONS:
(*Response:* Lord, hear our prayer.)
For employees and employers, that both may be able to settle
their differences in such a way that justice is served not
only for themselves but for all who are affected by

management and labor relations, let us pray to the Lord:
For families, that respect and consideration for the individual
human person be always maintained in the day-by-day
family activities so that decisions will be made for the
benefit of all members of the family, let us pray to the Lord:
For the peoples of all nations, that they not allow cultural
and nationalistic prejudices to prevent them from providing,
as only they can, the determination necessary among their
leaders to work for peace and cooperation, let us pray to
the Lord:
For each of us gathered here this day, that through close
friendships we come to an awareness of God and that we
provide the necessary means to become aware of God to
all whom we meet, let us pray to the Lord:

PERIOD OF REFLECTION:
Intermission

PROCESSIONAL:
"Behold Among Men," *Biblical Hymns and Psalms,* p. 36.

PRAYER OF BLESSING OVER GIFTS:
Only the "Let us pray that my sacrifice and yours . . ." and
its response is used today.

THE TABLE PRAYER

PREFACE:
"Table Prayer 2," *Open Your Hearts,* p. 11.

HYMN OF PRAISE:
"Holy, Holy, Holy! Lord God Almighty," *People's Mass Book,*
#184.

ACCLAMATION AT CONSECRATION:
"Keep in Mind," *People's Mass Book,* #145.

ENDING ACCLAMATION:
"Praise God, From Whom All Blessings Flow," *People's Mass
Book,* #45.

THE SERVICE OF COMMUNION

THE "OUR FATHER"

RITE OF PEACE

FRACTION RITE:
Litany of the "Lamb of God"

SONG:
"Whatsoever You Do," *People's Mass Book*, #208.

PERIOD OF REFLECTION:
Intermission

THE DISMISSAL RITE

PRAYER OF BENEDICTION:
We have heard your Word, O God.
We have broken bread together, hopefully,
  as a sign of friendship that exists and will continue to be.
As we meet the day with its many avenues of searching
  and as we explore the canyons of doubt,
  let us find in the companionship of men
  an inkling of the joy-filled life possible to us
  by our union with you.
We offer our hope-filled words to you, Father,
  as we search in Jesus' name,
  who with you and the Holy Spirit, lives as God,
  forever and ever.

BLESSING AND DISMISSAL

ANNOUNCEMENTS

RECESSIONAL:
"They'll Know We Are Christians," *Hymnal for Young Christians*, p. 132.

SECOND SUNDAY AFTER PENTECOST II

Theme: A People on the Way

THE ENTRANCE RITE

INVITATION TO WORSHIP:

Today we remind ourselves that the Church is a pilgrim and that God's life and love are not bound to the dimensions of this room. Let us pray together from our programs: "We thank you, God," *Your Word Is Near*, p. 149.

PROCESSIONAL:

"Alleluia! The Strife Is O'er," *People's Mass Book*, #34.

GREETING:

To all us pilgrims, travelers and refugees:
  grace be ours for a self-emptying in service;
  and peace from God our Father
  and from our brother, Jesus Christ,
  be with you all.

PRAYER OF INVOCATION:

We are your Church, Father, a people on the way.
We have a long past history, and we have a long way to go.
But in the now of things you gather us together
  to become a newer people,
  a community where we feed on the one food, Jesus Christ.
We pray that we may draw strength
  to feed the earth, filling its wants.
As your pilgrim people, we come to you in Jesus Christ,
  who is alive with us, forever and ever.

THE SERVICE OF THE WORD

FIRST READING:

1 Kings 19:4–8.

RESPONSE:
Galatians 2:16, 19–21. Introduction: For our response we read
the passage in which St. Paul speaks of the new food we
have for our journey through this world toward our Father's
house.

SECOND READING:
Omitted today.

GOSPEL ACCLAMATION:
"Your Word, O Lord," *Biblical Hymns and Psalms,* Vol. II,
p. 88. This is sung by the cantor; people respond with
"Alleluia, Alleluia," as indicated.

THE GOSPEL:
Luke 9:1–6.

GOSPEL ACCLAMATION:
"Alleluia, Alleluia," repeated from Gospel Acclamation above.

HOMILY

GENERAL INTENTIONS:
(*Response:* Lord, hear our prayer.)
Selection from pp. 36–37, *Your Word Is Near.*

PERIOD OF REFLECTION:
Intermission

PROCESSIONAL:
"Priestly People," *People's Mass Book,* #146.

PRAYER OF BLESSING OVER GIFTS:
Only the "Let us pray that my sacrifice and yours . . ." and
its response is used today.

THE TABLE PRAYER

PREFACE:
Gathered around your table, Father, we give you thanks
for your life and your love

and for bread shared in friendship,
for the wine of gladness—
for bread and wine in the hands of your Son Jesus.
For it was you who danced in the heavens, among the
sun, the moon and the stars.
It was you who established the earth by your breath and Word.
It was you who made us a people,
not to be idle, living for ourselves,
but to beautify and complete what you began,
to raise up cities from the ground
and sing new songs in the air.
In trying to make this city of man your kingdom,
you have given us a great thirst
which you satisfy in Jesus—one among us.
The risk, the loneliness, the possibility of failure,
the unknown nuances of life on the road,
the threat of no return
are the hardships we meet as your pilgrims.
But in Jesus we know the hint of promise, dim and
undetermined,
that something will come of our life, love, laughter, songs—
and that there is a good chance
that it will be enough for our world.
With all those reached and touched by each of us,
with those who fill the many crevices within us,
we praise you, our God, singing together now with one
voice:
(Adapted from "The Canon of the Pilgrim Church," *The
Experimental Liturgy Book*, p. 73.)

HYMN OF PRAISE:
"Now Thank We All Our God," third verse, *People's Mass
Book*, #178.

ACCLAMATION AT CONSECRATION:
#235a, *People's Mass Book*.

ENDING ACCLAMATION:
"You Alone Are Holy," *Biblical Hymns and Psalms*, Vol. II,
p. 52.

THE SERVICE OF COMMUNION

THE "OUR FATHER"

RITE OF PEACE

FRACTION RITE:
Litany of the "Lamb of God"

SONG:
"At the Lamb's High Feast," *Our Parish Prays and Sings,* #2.

PERIOD OF REFLECTION:
Intermission

THE DISMISSAL RITE

PRAYER OF BENEDICTION:
"We have heard your word, O God," *Your Word Is Near,* p. 123.

BLESSING AND DISMISSAL

ANNOUNCEMENTS

RECESSIONAL:
"Now Thank We All Our God," first verse, *People's Mass Book,* #178.

THIRD SUNDAY AFTER PENTECOST II

Theme: "You Are A Consecrated People"

THE ENTRANCE RITE

INVITATION TO WORSHIP:
In this morning's Gospel we will hear again the exciting words
of Jesus by which he commissioned the apostles to their
mission of reconciliation. It is a work begun in those twelve
and continued in us. For our own part, it is a work begun
at baptism and lived out in the service we render each other.
As the Israelites gathered to hear the Word of God and so
be consecrated by his presence, we gather this morning to
hear that Word and be made new. Listen now, and remember
again that what was said of these men of old is also said
of us. *(Here read Exodus 19:2–6a.)*

PROCESSIONAL:
"Priestly People," *Biblical Hymns and Psalms*, p. 74.

GREETING:
You are a consecrated people,
a holy nation, a people set apart!
May that grace and salvation of the Lord Jesus
be with you always.

PRAYER OF INVOCATION:
Conscious of the power of our God, we stand in awe
at his presence, and we pray:
You are praised and blest, our Father,
by all your creation.
May we, your people, gathered here before you,
find in this celebration
the strength to continually die to self
in order to rise
to the new life of your Son.
In Jesus' name we pray, today and forever and ever.

147

THE SERVICE OF THE WORD

FIRST READING:
Romans 5:6–11.

RESPONSE:
Silent reflection.

GOSPEL ACCLAMATION:
Repeat antiphon "Priestly People" from Processional.

THE GOSPEL:
Matthew 9:36–10:8.

GOSPEL ACCLAMATION:
Repeat from above.

HOMILY

GENERAL INTENTIONS

PERIOD OF REFLECTION:
Intermission

PROCESSIONAL

THE TABLE PRAYER

PREFACE:
See Fourth Sunday of Easter II, this volume.

HYMN OF PRAISE:
"Holy, Holy, Holy" to any melody familiar to congregation.

ACCLAMATION AT CONSECRATION:
#139b, *People's Mass Book.*

ENDING ACCLAMATION:
"Praise God from Whom All Blessings Flow," *People's Mass Book,* #45.

THE SERVICE OF COMMUNION

THE "OUR FATHER"

RITE OF PEACE

FRACTION RITE:
Litany of the "Lamb of God"

SONG:
"Glorify the Lord with Me," *Biblical Hymns and Psalms*, p. 78.

PERIOD OF REFLECTION:
Intermission

THE DISMISSAL RITE

PRAYER OF BENEDICTION:
You have entrusted us with the mission
of bringing your kingdom to those
who are lost and disillusioned.
We remember all your saving deeds
done on our behalf; therefore in faith
we reach out in confidence to one another
and we praise you by our lives together.
In Jesus' name we have prayed and broken bread,
and in his name we continue to live, forever and ever.

BLESSING AND DISMISSAL

ANNOUNCEMENTS

RECESSIONAL:
"Behold Among Men," *Biblical Hymns and Psalms*, p. 36.

FOURTH SUNDAY AFTER PENTECOST II

Theme: The Cross of Discipleship

THE ENTRANCE RITE

INVITATION TO WORSHIP:
At the Eucharist today we reflect on the vocation of the
prophet and the suffering which that vocation seems to carry
with it. The Word of God is never easily received, and the
bearer of that Word suffers much to let that Word become
flesh. He suffers in himself as he commits himself to his own
conversion, and he suffers at the hands of those to whom he
seeks to bring salvation. In the midst of this suffering the true
prophet can only turn to God for his help. So we begin today
by praying together a lament from the psalter; then we will
spend a few moments calling to mind the times we have
ridiculed the prophets in our midst and the times we've
suffered from the scorn of others as we sought to share in the
prophetic role of God's people. *(Here read Psalm 69:5–9,
16–18, 32–34.)*

PROCESSIONAL:
"My Soul Is Longing," *People's Mass Book*, #161.

GREETING:
We gather to pray, to be re-created
in strength by the saving power of God's Word.
May the Spirit that brings the vigor of new life
be with you all.

PRAYER OF INVOCATION:
Conscious of our weakness and of our failures in the
face of trouble, we pray:
Your Son knew the weight of your Word, our Father.
He suffered rejection and loneliness
as well as discouragement in his own heart.
Like him we cry to you
for your aid and your presence.
In the faith you have given us

150

we find strength,
and in the Eucharist he left us
we find a measure of his peace.
Refresh us now in him
as we pray in the name of your Son, Jesus,
who lives forever and ever.

THE SERVICE OF THE WORD

FIRST READING:
Jeremiah 20:10–13.

RESPONSE:
"I Lift Up My Eyes," *Twenty-Four Psalms and a Canticle*,
p. 40.

THE GOSPEL:
Matthew 10:26–33.

HOMILY

GENERAL INTENTIONS

PERIOD OF REFLECTION:
Intermission

PROCESSIONAL

THE TABLE PRAYER

PREFACE:
As given in Commentary, Robert W. Hovda, *Manual of
Celebration*, p. 28. May be abbreviated by leaving out
section beginning "status of sons" and ending "giving us
your splendor."

HYMN OF PRAISE:
"Holy, Holy, Holy," to any melody known by congregation.

ACCLAMATION AT CONSECRATION:
"Without Seeing You," *People's Mass Book*, #173.

ENDING ACCLAMATION:
"You Alone Are Holy," *Biblical Hymns and Psalms*, Vol. II, p. 52.

THE SERVICE OF COMMUNION

THE "OUR FATHER"

RITE OF PEACE

FRACTION RITE:
Litany of the "Lamb of God"

SONG:
"My Shepherd Is the Lord," *Twenty-Four Psalms and a Canticle*, p. 10.

PERIOD OF REFLECTION:
Intermission

THE DISMISSAL RITE

PRAYER OF BENEDICTION:
There is hope for us even in our failures, Lord,
    because by this sacrament you are with us.
By your Word read and proclaimed, lived and suffered,
    we are made new, made young and strong.
May you be blessed by our service and our love
    in the days to come.
In Jesus' name we pray, now and forever and ever.

BLESSING AND DISMISSAL

ANNOUNCEMENTS

RECESSIONAL:
"The Church's One Foundation," *People's Mass Book*, #223.

FIFTH SUNDAY AFTER PENTECOST II

Theme: The Beatitude of Discipleship

THE ENTRANCE RITE

INVITATION TO WORSHIP:
Paragraph beginning "Therefore Jesus calls his disciples
blessed. . . ," p. 118 of Dietrich Bonhoeffer, *The Cost of
Discipleship.*

PROCESSIONAL:
"My Soul Is Longing," *People's Mass Book*, #161.

GREETING:
For those who anticipate with joy
the Word of God with its peace and its hope.
I wish blessings and that the Lord be with you.

PRAYER OF INVOCATION:
Mindful that the dwelling of the Word among men is to
make us free, we pray:
God our Father, to free us from the demands
of this world for the sake of your kingdom,
you sent us your Son
who taught us how to live here.
He said that those who were poor were blessed,
and to be found happy in your kingdom.
By our faith we search
for our place in the kingdom;
confessing our needs we make ourselves poor
for service and pilgrimage.
In Jesus' name we are one
and we gather to pray this day
and in the days to come forever and ever.

THE SERVICE OF THE WORD

FIRST READING:
1 Corinthians 1:26–31.

RESPONSE:
   The paragraph immediately following the passage cited in
the Invitation to Worship may be printed on the program
for silent reflection at this time.

SECOND READING:
   Zephaniah 2:3; 3:12–13.

GOSPEL ACCLAMATION:
   "Your Word, O Lord," *Biblical Hymns and Psalms,* Vol. II,
p. 88.

THE GOSPEL:
   Matthew 5:1–12a.

GOSPEL ACCLAMATION:
   Repeat from above.

HOMILY

GENERAL INTENTIONS

PERIOD OF REFLECTION:
   Intermission

PROCESSIONAL

THE TABLE PRAYER

PREFACE:
   "Canon of the Love of God," *The Experimental Liturgy Book,*
p. 102.

HYMN OF PRAISE

ACCLAMATION AT CONSECRATION:
   #235a, *People's Mass Book.*

ENDING ACCLAMATION:
   #190b, *People's Mass Book.*

THE SERVICE OF COMMUNION

THE "OUR FATHER"

RITE OF PEACE

FRACTION RITE:
Litany of the "Lamb of God"

SONG:
"Longing for God," *Biblical Hymns and Psalms,* p. 100.

PERIOD OF REFLECTION:
Intermission

THE DISMISSAL RITE

PRAYER OF BENEDICTION:
With nothing were we born, Lord our Father,
and it is in this condition
that we must approach your kingdom,
rejecting the baggage of sin,
of selfishness, of ambition and power.
Like your Son, we may come to you,
recognizing our needs,
seeking only the glory of your name,
a name that is peace, that is unity, that is joy.
All glory be to you Father,
through your Son Jesus
who with the Spirit unites us in hope, forever and ever.

BLESSING AND DISMISSAL

ANNOUNCEMENTS

RECESSIONAL:
"Behold Among Men," *Biblical Hymns and Psalms,* p. 36.

SIXTH SUNDAY AFTER PENTECOST II

Theme: Savior of the Poor

THE ENTRANCE RITE

INVITATION TO WORSHIP:
> In the liturgy today we call to mind the images of the
> Messiah given to us by the prophets, recalling the Son of
> God as sent to the poor. In his own chosen reading at the
> synagogue of his home town he announced his purpose as
> having come to set the captives free, to give sight to the
> blind. Not sent to the rich and satisfied, he came to the poor,
> the lonely, the sick, the abandoned, bringing to all the message
> of peace. *(Here read Psalm 72:1–4, 12–13, 7–8, 17.)*

PROCESSIONAL

GREETING:
> We gather to give praise to the God of Israel,
>> who has worked wonders through all ages.
> In his Son, Jesus, he has brought us peace.
> May the Spirit of that Lord and Savior,
>> risen from the dead, be with you all.

PRAYER OF INVOCATION:
> Conscious of our slavery to sin and selfishness, and therefore
> our need for the saving presence of Christ the Lord, let us
> pray:
> You have sent your Son to us, our Father,
>> to free us from our past.
> In our poverty and our sinfulness
>> we cry out *"Abba"*—"Father."
> In joy we give thanks
>> for the hope you have given,
>> for the comfort of this Eucharist,
>> and for the Spirit which draws us to you.
> In the name of Jesus we pray,
>> now and forever and ever.

THE SERVICE OF THE WORD

FIRST READING:
Zechariah 9:9–10.

RESPONSE:
Psalm 145:1–4, 13b, 21.

GOSPEL ACCLAMATION

THE GOSPEL:
Matthew 11:25–30.

GOSPEL ACCLAMATION

HOMILY

GENERAL INTENTIONS

PERIOD OF REFLECTION:
Intermission

PROCESSIONAL

THE TABLE PRAYER

PREFACE:
As in Commentary, *Manual of Celebration*, p. 33.

HYMN OF PRAISE

ACCLAMATION AT CONSECRATION

ENDING ACCLAMATION

THE SERVICE OF COMMUNION

THE "OUR FATHER"

RITE OF PEACE

FRACTION RITE:
   Litany of the "Lamb of God"

SONG

PERIOD OF REFLECTION:
   Intermission

THE DISMISSAL RITE

PRAYER OF BENEDICTION:
   May this Eucharist preserve in us
      the peace your Son has left us.
   The fellowship and the promise of life
      are our strength and our hope
      as we seek to serve those given into our care.
   May you be blessed and praised, our Father,
      by all we do with the help of your Son.
   It is in his name that we pray, today and forever.

BLESSING AND DISMISSAL

ANNOUNCEMENTS

RECESSIONAL

SEVENTH SUNDAY AFTER PENTECOST II

Theme: Promise of Harvest

THE ENTRANCE RITE

INVITATION TO WORSHIP:

In today's liturgy we are going to join the whole of creation, and especially the whole Church, in giving thanks to the Father for the seed of faith sown in our hearts by his gracious love. We ponder the Word of God to reassess our own growth in faith and in truth as we seek continually to be of better service to one another in the effort to reap a harvest of love and peace in the kingdom of the Father. St. Paul wrote to the Church at Corinth in these terms. *(Here read 2 Corinthians 9:10-15.)*

PROCESSIONAL:

"Praise to the Holiest," *People's Mass Book*, #179.

GREETING:

Peace be with you.

PRAYER OF INVOCATION:

There is power beyond our imagination in the Word of God made flesh—power to raise the dead to life, power to lift us beyond our fumbling and perfect our faltering sacrifice. In that hope and with joy, we pray:
We proclaim your Son in our community,
  and we praise you, God our Father,
  for the perfection of humanness
  and for the hope you give us in him.
We remember him now
  as he asked to be remembered
  in unity and peace at the table.
We break bread to proclaim your glory.
In Jesus' name we pray forever and ever.

THE SERVICE OF THE WORD

FIRST READING:
Isaiah 55:10–11.

RESPONSE:
Isaiah 55:12–13.

SECOND READING

GOSPEL ACCLAMATION:
Psalm 65:8–13. Followed by a sung "Alleluia."

THE GOSPEL:
Matthew 13:1–23.

GOSPEL ACCLAMATION:
Repeat from above.

HOMILY

GENERAL INTENTIONS

PERIOD OF REFLECTION:
Intermission

PROCESSIONAL

THE TABLE PRAYER

PREFACE:
It is fitting for our salvation, God, our almighty Father,
that your gracious deeds done for us
be recalled and proclaimed;
for you have taken us from our loneliness
and by your Son Jesus Christ
you have called us all sons and daughters
and given us a place in your kingdom.
Your Word is power and light,
and it is that Word, present in our midst,
that gives us courage and consolation.

It is that Word taking flesh again in us
   that fills us with joy
   as we look for the day
   when your kingdom will finally break open
   for all men.   Until that time,
   we break bread and break our own lives
   that we may live.
With hope in your promise we join all creation
   in singing a hymn to your praise:

HYMN OF PRAISE:
   "Praise God from Whom All Blessings Flow," *People's Mass Book*, #45.

ACCLAMATION AT CONSECRATION:
   "Keep in Mind," *People's Mass Book*, #145.

ENDING ACCLAMATION:
   "Amen" sung to any melody known to congregation.

THE SERVICE OF COMMUNION

THE "OUR FATHER"

RITE OF PEACE

FRACTION RITE:
   Litany of the "Lamb of God"

SONG

PERIOD OF REFLECTION:
   Intermission

THE DISMISSAL RITE

PRAYER OF BENEDICTION:
   "God in Our Worried Hearts," *Tender of Wishes*, p. 136.

BLESSING AND DISMISSAL

ANNOUNCEMENTS

RECESSIONAL:
"Now Thank We All Our God," *People's Mass Book*, #178.

EIGHTH SUNDAY AFTER PENTECOST II

Theme: The Smallest of All the Seeds

THE ENTRANCE RITE

INVITATION TO WORSHIP:
With today's liturgy we are in the middle of a three-Sunday
series of readings and prayer over the kingdom of God as
offered by the parables in the 13th chapter of St. Matthew's
Gospel. With the parable of the sower last Sunday we
introduced the subject and considered the mystery of God's
decision to speak to us in parable form, making the meaning
a riddle to those who are not faithful. Contemplating the
parable of the weeds and the wheat, we reconsidered the
same theme in parable form, reminding ourselves that not
everything is always what it seems to be; that the particular
weed in the parable looks much like wheat, and the two
can often be confused—not everyone who recites creeds is
necessarily going to find a place in the kingdom of the Father.
It is the Father himself who will ultimately choose his own.
In today's celebration we will try to find our place in God's
plan. With patience and humility we reflect on our ability
to compromise and weaken the Word of God. By counting
ourselves among those who need his saving presence we
hope to give rise to a new spirit of conversion and experience
a resurrection of new life for ourselves individually and as a
community.

PROCESSIONAL:
"Happy the Man," *People's Mass Book*, #214.

GREETING:
To you who gather in humility
    to hear God's Word of hope
    and to count yourselves among those
    who are in need of his mercy and his strength—
I pray that the Lord may be with you.

PRAYER OF INVOCATION:
In the words of the Book of Wisdom I pray:
(Wisdom 12:13–18)
We praise you in the name of your Son, Jesus Christ
the Lord, now and forever and ever.

THE SERVICE OF THE WORD

FIRST READING:
Ezekiel 17:22–24.

RESPONSE:
Psalm 86:5–6, 9–10, 16b–17a.

GOSPEL ACCLAMATION

THE GOSPEL:
Matthew 13:31–35.

GOSPEL ACCLAMATION

HOMILY

PROFESSION OF FAITH

GENERAL INTENTIONS

PERIOD OF REFLECTION:
Intermission

PROCESSIONAL

THE TABLE PRAYER

PREFACE:
As in Commentary, *Manual of Celebration*, p. 36.

HYMN OF PRAISE:
"Praise, My Soul, the King of Heaven," *People's Mass Book*,
#183.

ACCLAMATION AT CONSECRATION:
"Keep in Mind," *People's Mass Book,* #145.

ENDING ACCLAMATION:
"Amen" to any melody known to congregation.

THE SERVICE OF COMMUNION

THE "OUR FATHER"

RITE OF PEACE

FRACTION RITE:
Litany of the "Lamb of God"

READING FOR MEDITATION:
Romans 11:16–18.

THE DISMISSAL RITE

PRAYER OF BENEDICTION:
"We have heard your word, O God," *Your Word Is Near,*
p. 123.

BLESSING AND DISMISSAL

ANNOUNCEMENTS

RECESSIONAL

NINTH SUNDAY AFTER PENTECOST II

Theme: "Nothing Can Separate Us from the Love of God"

THE ENTRANCE RITE

INVITATION TO WORSHIP:

We conclude three Sundays of prayerful reflection upon the parables of the kingdom today. Some light for understanding these parables in the context of today's celebration comes from Paul's letter to the Romans. (Here read Romans 8:18–27.)

PROCESSIONAL:

"My Soul Is Thirsting for the Lord," *Twenty-Four Psalms and a Canticle*, p. 16.

GREETING:

To you who wait for the Lord in patience and in peace,
I bring the Word of God, the Word made flesh.

PRAYER OF INVOCATION:

Let us pray for the Spirit, that he may give us words to express our faith in our weakness:
Father, you know all things;
give us again your Spirit
to keep us together and in faith,
as we wait for your glory.
We give you praise and thanksgiving
through your Son Jesus forever.

THE SERVICE OF THE WORD

FIRST READING:

Romans 8:28–39.

RESPONSE:

Paul Tillich in *Horizons of Hope*, p. 165.

GOSPEL ACCLAMATION:
"Your Word, O Lord," *Biblical Hymns and Psalms*, Vol. II, p. 88.

THE GOSPEL:
Matthew 13:44–52.

GOSPEL ACCLAMATION:
Repeat from above.

HOMILY

GENERAL INTENTIONS

PERIOD OF REFLECTION:
Intermission

PROCESSIONAL

THE TABLE PRAYER

PREFACE:
See Second Sunday of Easter II, this volume.

HYMN OF PRAISE:
"Holy, Holy, Holy" to any melody known to congregation.

ACCLAMATION AT CONSECRATION:
"Without Seeing You," People's Mass Book, #173.

ENDING ACCLAMATION:
"You Alone Are Holy," *Biblical Hymns and Psalms*, Vol. II, p. 52.

THE SERVICE OF COMMUNION

THE "OUR FATHER"

RITE OF PEACE

FRACTION RITE:
Litany of the "Lamb of God"

READING FOR MEDITATION:
Daniel 4:7–14.

THE DISMISSAL RITE

PRAYER OF BENEDICTION:
"God, it is your happiness and life," *Your Word Is Near*, p. 96.

BLESSING AND DISMISSAL

ANNOUNCEMENTS

RECESSIONAL:
"You Fill the Day," *People's Mass Book*, #203.

TENTH SUNDAY AFTER PENTECOST II

Theme: The Transfiguration

THE ENTRANCE RITE

INVITATION TO WORSHIP:
Today's festival gives us cause to reflect on the glory of the
Son of God—the Word made flesh. We consider the glory of
Christ in the very midst of his incarnate life. It is a glory
that is part of his being man, in the flesh; it is not a glory
that somehow splits his existence and makes his presence
somehow unreal or transcendent. It is Christ the human,
the flesh and blood that is glorified. The transfiguration reveals
Jesus in his earthly existence as the one who is to be exalted
as the Son of Man after his suffering.

PROCESSIONAL:
"Crown Him with Many Crowns," *People's Mass Book*, #49.

GREETING:
May the victory and the spirit
of the triumphant and risen Son of God
be with you all.

PRAYER OF INVOCATION:
"Eternal God, we bear your name, your imprint," *Your Word
Is Near*, p. 61.

THE SERVICE OF THE WORD

FIRST READING:
Daniel 7:9–10, 13–14.

RESPONSE:
Silent reflection; then Psalm 97:1–2, 5–6, 9.

SECOND READING
2 Peter 1:16–19.

GOSPEL ACCLAMATION:
   "Your Word, O Lord," *Biblical Hymns and Psalms,* Vol. II,
   p. 88.

THE GOSPEL:
   Matthew 17:1–9.

GOSPEL ACCLAMATION:
   Repeat from above.

HOMILY

GENERAL INTENTIONS

PERIOD OF REFLECTION:
   Intermission

PROCESSIONAL

THE TABLE PRAYER

PREFACE:
   See Preface, Second Sunday of Lent II, this volume.

HYMN OF PRAISE:
   "Holy, Holy, Holy! Lord God Almighty," *People's Mass Book,*
   #184.

ACCLAMATION AT CONSECRATION:
   "Keep in Mind," *People's Mass Book,* #145, antiphon with
   first two verses.

ENDING ACCLAMATION

THE SERVICE OF COMMUNION

THE "OUR FATHER"

RITE OF PEACE

FRACTION RITE:
  Litany of the "Lamb of God"

SONG

PERIOD OF REFLECTION:
  Intermission

THE DISMISSAL RITE

PRAYER OF BENEDICTION:
  You have touched us again through your Son Jesus Christ.
  He has risen from the dead,
    and we have broken bread in his memory.
  The time has come
    for us to tell all men of the vision we have—
    to tell them of your glory
    and the glory that awaits those
    who have faith in your presence.
  May we persevere in service, strengthened by this meal,
    announcing your love and showing your glory.
  In Jesus' name we pray, today and forever and ever.

BLESSING AND DISMISSAL

ANNOUNCEMENTS

RECESSIONAL:
  "All Glory, Praise, and Honor," *People's Mass Book*, #29.

ELEVENTH SUNDAY AFTER PENTECOST II

Theme: The Double-Minded Man Receives Nothing from the Lord

THE ENTRANCE RITE

INVITATION TO WORSHIP:
In today's liturgy we prayerfully consider the Gospel story
of the calming of storm by Jesus' approach, walking on the
waters. We call to mind the image of the Church as a ship.
And how fragile a ship it is, fashioned out of humanity! Like
the ship, whenever the Church ventures out, daring to be
what it must be, it is tossed and endangered by storms of
protest and reaction; yet it must make this risk. Christ's only
rebuke comes because of little faith. Like Peter (perhaps
for us a symbol of the Church) we are called to have faith
and trust in Jesus.

PROCESSIONAL:
"The Church's One Foundation," *People's Mass Book*, #223.

GREETING:
Peace be with you who are called
to believe and to trust in times of difficulty.

PRAYER OF INVOCATION:
Mindful of our own weakness and our too frequent
contributions to the confusion and suffering of others, let us
pray:
Be with us now, our Father, as we gather
in the name of your Son, Jesus.
We break bread in his memory,
becoming new people,
willing to live in difficult times
in order to share in his resurrection.
All glory be yours, in his name,
now and forever and ever.

THE SERVICE OF THE WORD

FIRST READING:
1 Kings 19:4–13a.

GOSPEL ACCLAMATION:
"Your Word, O Lord," *Biblical Hymns and Psalms*, Vol. II,
p. 88.

THE GOSPEL:
Matthew 14:22–33.

GOSPEL ACCLAMATION:
Repeat from above.

HOMILY

GENERAL INTENTIONS

PERIOD OF REFLECTION:
Intermission

PROCESSIONAL

THE TABLE PRAYER

PREFACE:
See Second Sunday after Pentecost II, this volume.

HYMN OF PRAISE:
"Now Thank We All Our God," *People's Mass Book*, #178.

ACCLAMATION AT CONSECRATION

ENDING ACCLAMATION

THE SERVICE OF COMMUNION

THE "OUR FATHER"

RITE OF PEACE

FRACTION RITE:
   Litany of the "Lamb of God"

PERIOD OF REFLECTION:
   The following "creed" is read by all: "We have been fed and
   strengthened," in *He Is the Still Point of the Turning World*,
   p. 89.

THE DISMISSAL RITE

PRAYER OF BENEDICTION

BLESSING AND DISMISSAL

ANNOUNCEMENTS

RECESSIONAL:
   "Father We Thank Thee," *People's Mass Book*, #177.

TWELFTH SUNDAY AFTER PENTECOST II

Theme: The Narrow Door

THE ENTRANCE RITE

INVITATION TO WORSHIP:
Pierre Babin in *Listen to Love,* p. 83. The last sentence may be
read by all.

PROCESSIONAL:
"All the Earth," *Biblical Hymns and Psalms,* p. 72.

GREETING:
Blessings to you who come in peace
    to hear God's Word
    and to find your place in his kingdom
    regardless of the cost.
May the Spirit of the Lord triumphant be with you.

PRAYER OF INVOCATION:
"You are the voice of the living God," *Your Word Is Near,*
p. 97.

THE SERVICE OF THE WORD

FIRST READING:
Isaiah 66:18–21.

RESPONSE:
"Be glad and remember the Lord here among us" (all four
stanzas), *Prayers, Poems & Songs,* p. 28.

SECOND READING:
Hebrews 12:5–7.

GOSPEL ACCLAMATION:
"Alleluia! Alleluia!," *Biblical Hymns and Psalms,* p. 86.

THE GOSPEL:
Luke 13:22–30.

GOSPEL ACCLAMATION:
Repeat from above.

HOMILY

PERIOD OF REFLECTION:
Intermission

PROCESSIONAL

THE TABLE PRAYER

PREFACE:
#2, *Open Your Hearts*, p. 11.

HYMN OF PRAISE

ACCLAMATION AT CONSECRATION

ENDING ACCLAMATION

THE SERVICE OF COMMUNION

THE "OUR FATHER"

RITE OF PEACE

FRACTION RITE:
Litany of the "Lamb of God"

SONG

PERIOD OF REFLECTION:
Intermission

THE DISMISSAL RITE

PRAYER OF BENEDICTION:
"You have kindled," *Your Word Is Near*, p. 103.

BLESSING AND DISMISSAL

ANNOUNCEMENTS

RECESSIONAL

THIRTEENTH SUNDAY AFTER PENTECOST II

Theme: Humility through Self-Knowledge

THE ENTRANCE RITE

INVITATION TO WORSHIP:
> First paragraph, "Preface," *Shaping of a Self;* then people join in reading the following: Karl Rahner in *Faces of Freedom,* p. 180.

PROCESSIONAL

GREETING:
> Blessings to you who gather together
>> to be fed and strengthened
>> by the Word made flesh
>> for your growth in self-knowledge and in the Spirit.
> May the Spirit of the Lord be with you.

PRAYER OF INVOCATION:
> "God, we have not seen your Son," *Your Word Is Near,* p. 95.

THE SERVICE OF THE WORD

FIRST READING:
> Ecclesiasticus 3:17(19)–20(21), 28(30)–29(31).

RESPONSE:
> Dag Hammarskjold in *Shaping of a Self,* p. 70.

SECOND READING:
> Hebrews 12:18–19, 22–24.

GOSPEL ACCLAMATION:
> "Alleluia! Alleluia!," *Biblical Hymns and Psalms,* p. 86.

THE GOSPEL:
> Luke 14:1, 7–14.

GOSPEL ACCLAMATION:
   Repeat from above.

HOMILY

GENERAL INTENTIONS

PERIOD OF REFLECTION:
   Intermission

PROCESSIONAL

THE TABLE PRAYER

PREFACE:
   #3, *Open Your Hearts*, p. 15.

HYMN OF PRAISE

ACCLAMATION AT CONSECRATION:
   #235a, *People's Mass Book.*

ENDING ACCLAMATION:
   "Praise God, From Whom All Blessings Flow," *People's Mass Book*, #45.

THE SERVICE OF COMMUNION

THE "OUR FATHER"

RITE OF PEACE

FRACTION RITE:
   Litany of the "Lamb of God"

MEDITATION:
   Abraham Maslow in *Shaping of a Self*, p. 63.

THE DISMISSAL RITE

PRAYER OF BENEDICTION:
"We are as you have made us," *Your Word Is Near,* p. 94.

BLESSING AND DISMISSAL

ANNOUNCEMENTS

RECESSIONAL

FOURTEENTH SUNDAY AFTER PENTECOST II

Theme: A Forgiving Father: Cause To Celebrate

THE ENTRANCE RITE

INVITATION TO WORSHIP:
   As members of God's family and as sharers in this assembly
   of believers we gather here in faith, admitting that at times
   we grow weary—weary of ourselves, of one another, yes, even
   of God himself. We try so hard and yet accomplish so little.
   And it seems sometimes that the more we try to do what is
   right and according to Christ's teachings, the more we seem
   to fall into sin. But may that not be the paradox of the
   Christian life? The more closely we seek to be identified with
   Jesus Christ, the more we see what there is to be done in
   ourselves and in our world. Thus, we gather here in faith—
   believing in the power of Christ's love and the strength of
   his Spirit—and we pledge once again by our honest confession
   of our shortcomings that we will seek to be ever more closely
   identified with the Lord Jesus. In this spirit let us stand and
   sing of our faith.

PROCESSIONAL:
   "Keep in Mind," *People's Mass Book*, #145.

GREETING:
   Blessings and peace to you who have come here
      seeking the way and the truth—
      a way which brings us up from our past,
      and a truth which makes us one with the Father
      who offers us his life.
   May the forgiving and healing Lord Jesus be with you.

PENITENTIAL RITE:
   Ashes may be distributed at this time; see note at Blessing
   and Dismissal.

PRAYER OF INVOCATION:
   God our Father, through the Word of your Son Jesus,

181

you have taught us
that our prayer of thanksgiving to you
has no meaning if we come here
without first being reconciled with our brother.
So we come here asking you
to give us the strength we need
to seek forgiveness and also to forgive those
who ask forgiveness of us.
Father, give us the courage and determination
to try once more to live
as Jesus himself has taught us.
We ask this in his name
who with you and the Holy Spirit
lives as God, forever and ever.

THE SERVICE OF THE WORD

FIRST READING:
Reuel L. Howe in *Listen to Love*, p. 95.

RESPONSE:
Help me, O God, since I do not understand my own actions,
for I do not do what I want, but I do the
very thing I hate.
I can will what is right, but I cannot do it.
For I do not do the good I want.
(Adapted from Romans 7:15–19.)

GOSPEL ACCLAMATION:
"Grant to Us," *Biblical Hymns and Psalms*, p. 40.

THE GOSPEL:
Luke 15:11–24.

GOSPEL ACCLAMATION:
Repeat from above.

HOMILY:
Examination of conscience, hearing of confessions, and
absolution may follow if desired.

PERIOD OF REFLECTION:
Intermission

PROCESSIONAL:
"Peace I Leave With You," *Hymnal for Young Christians,*
Vol. II, Congregation Edition, p. 34.

THE TABLE PRAYER

PREFACE:
"Canon of Christian Service," in *The Experimental Liturgy
Book,* p. 66, through the words "in suffering and in joy."
Continue with #208, "Eternal God, our judge and redeemer
. . ." in *The Experimental Liturgy Book.* If this liturgy is
being used as a penance service, substitute the words of
absolution for the last sentence, "I declare to you. . . ."

ACCLAMATION AT CONSECRATION:
#235a, *People's Mass Book.*

ENDING ACCLAMATION:
"You Alone Are Holy," *Biblical Hymns and Psalms,* Vol. II,
p. 52.

THE SERVICE OF COMMUNION

THE "OUR FATHER"

RITE OF PEACE

FRACTION RITE:
Litany of the "Lamb of God"

SONG:
"God Is Love," any arrangement known to congregation.

PERIOD OF REFLECTION:
Intermission

THE DISMISSAL RITE

PRAYER OF BENEDICTION:
   "You have made your dwelling," *Your Word Is Near*, p. 139.

BLESSING AND DISMISSAL:
   If ashes have been distributed, at this point (or right after
   absolution if the sacrament of penance has been administered),
   the celebrant asks the members of the congregation to turn
   to one another and, as a sign that "the forgiveness of the
   Father is alive in us," wipe away the ashes, the sign of sin,
   from each other's forehead.

ANNOUNCEMENTS

RECESSIONAL:
   "They'll Know We Are Christians," *Hymnal for Young
   Christians* Vol. II, Congregation Edition, p. 39.

FIFTEENTH SUNDAY AFTER PENTECOST II

Theme: What It Means To Be a "Tent People"

THE ENTRANCE RITE

INVITATION TO WORSHIP:
Herman Hesse in *Listen to Love*, p. 184.

PROCESSIONAL:
"Without Seeing You," *People's Mass Book*, #173.

GREETING:
Eucharistic Liturgies, p. 99.

PRAYER OF INVOCATION:
Eucharistic Liturgies, p. 99.

THE SERVICE OF THE WORD

FIRST READING:
Jeremiah 17:5-8.

RESPONSE:
Jeremiah 16:19-21.

SECOND READING:
2 Corinthians 5:1-5.

GOSPEL ACCLAMATION:
"Alleluia! Alleluia!," *Biblical Hymns and Psalms*, p. 86.

THE GOSPEL:
Luke 14:25-33.

GOSPEL ACCLAMATION:
Repeat from above.

HOMILY

GENERAL INTENTIONS

PERIOD OF REFLECTION:
   Intermission

PROCESSIONAL

THE TABLE PRAYER

PREFACE:
   "The Canon of the Pilgrim Church," in *The Experimental Liturgy Book*, p. 73.

HYMN OF PRAISE:
   "Praise, My Soul, the King of Heaven," *People's Mass Book*, #183.

ACCLAMATION AT CONSECRATION:
   #190b, *People's Mass Book*.

ENDING ACCLAMATION:
   Repeat from above.

THE SERVICE OF COMMUNION

THE "OUR FATHER"

RITE OF PEACE

FRACTION RITE:
   Litany of the "Lamb of God"

SONG:
   "Lamb of God," *People's Mass Book*, #116.

PERIOD OF REFLECTION:
   Intermission

THE DISMISSAL RITE

PRAYER OF BENEDICTION:

Eucharistic Liturgies, p. 100, beginning with "Help us to know what it is. . . ."

BLESSING AND DISMISSAL

ANNOUNCEMENTS

RECESSIONAL:

"O God, Our Help in Ages Past," *People's Mass Book,* #185.

SIXTEENTH SUNDAY AFTER PENTECOST II

Theme: The Cry of the Poor: Who Will Listen?

THE ENTRANCE RITE

INVITATION TO WORSHIP:
"This Still Young World of Ours," *Tender of Wishes*, p. 109.

PROCESSIONAL:
"Draw Near, O Lord," *People's Mass Book*, #22.

GREETING:
Blessings to you who are in turmoil
    and turn to God's World made flesh for hope.
May the Spirit of Christ risen be your light.

PRAYER OF INVOCATION:
Remembering that as long as one man suffers, the Body of
Christ of which we are members can have no rest—and that
suffering must touch us all, we pray: *Continue with* "Father,
you have put us on this earth," *Eucharistic Liturgies*, p. 117.

THE SERVICE OF THE WORD

FIRST READING:
Martin Luther King in *Horizons of Hope*, p. 84.

RESPONSE:
"Prayer for Untroubled People," *Tender of Wishes*, p. 30–31.
After first four lines, skip to "Coax them out of hiding. . . ."

GOSPEL ACCLAMATION:
"Alleluia! Alleluia!," *Biblical Hymns and Psalms*, p. 86.

THE GOSPEL:
Luke 16:1–13.

GOSPEL ACCLAMATION:
Repeat from above.

HOMILY

CREEDAL RESPONSE:
"We believe in God, and the goodness of all his creation" through "Without him there can be no love, no hunger, no desire," from Thomas Wolfe in script for CBS program "When Men and Mountains Meet" by Joe McCarthy.

GENERAL INTENTIONS

PERIOD OF REFLECTION:
Intermission

PROCESSIONAL

THE TABLE PRAYER

PREFACE:
"Canon of Christian Service," in *The Experimental Liturgy Book*, p. 66.

HYMN OF PRAISE:
"Holy, Holy, Holy," *People's Mass Book*, #106.

ACCLAMATION AT CONSECRATION:
#190b, *People's Mass Book*.

ENDING ACCLAMATION:
"Amen," to any melody familiar to congregation.

THE SERVICE OF COMMUNION

THE "OUR FATHER"

RITE OF PEACE

FRACTION RITE:
Litany of the "Lamb of God"

SONG:
"There Is One Lord," *People's Mass Book*, #168.

PERIOD OF REFLECTION:
  Intermission

THE DISMISSAL RITE

PRAYER OF BENEDICTION:
  By our oneness and our common suffering, eternal Father,
    keep us from becoming hard and cold to the needs
    which cry to you for justice.
  Let our ears be yours;
    use us as the agent of your mercy
    to bring comfort to the suffering
    and to soothe the hurts which surround us.
  We thank you
    that you have not left us alone in our misery,
    but by your Son you have caused us to see
    that we must face wrong everywhere.
  Help us to thaw frozen hearts,
    to remember that the future lies
    not anywhere but in ourselves.
  It is in the name of your only Son Jesus
    that we pray in his Spirit,
    forever and ever.

BLESSING AND DISMISSAL:
  #901 in *The Experimental Liturgy Book*, p. 126.

ANNOUNCEMENTS

RECESSIONAL:
  "At the Lamb's High Feast," *Our Parish Prays and Sings*,
  #2.

SEVENTEENTH SUNDAY AFTER PENTECOST II

Theme: Mercy: God's Word Active Among Us

THE ENTRANCE RITE

INVITATION TO WORSHIP:
"i am a little church," *95 Poems.*

PROCESSIONAL:
"Sion, Sing, Break Into Song," *People's Mass Book,* #165.

GREETING:
Grace and blessings from our Father who calls us
to follow his Son wholeheartedly
and thus find our true happiness.

PRAYER OF INVOCATION:
"You called us with your voice," *Your Word Is Near,* p. 145.

THE SERVICE OF THE WORD

FIRST READING:
Hebrews 4:12–16.

RESPONSE:
John 1:1, 2–5, 9–10, 11–12a, 14, alternated with John 8:31–32.

SECOND READING:
Ephesians 4:1–13.

GOSPEL ACCLAMATION:
"Alleluia! Alleluia!," *Biblical Hymns and Psalms,* p. 86.

THE GOSPEL:
Luke 8:19–21.

GOSPEL ACCLAMATION:
Repeat from above.

HOMILY

PROFESSION OF FAITH:
  Mission Creed (see Second Sunday of Easter II, this
  volume).

GENERAL INTENTIONS

PERIOD OF REFLECTION:
  Intermission

PROCESSIONAL

THE TABLE PRAYER

PREFACE:
  "Canon of Christian Service," in *The Experimental Liturgy
  Book*, p. 66.

HYMN OF PRAISE:
  "Holy, Holy, Holy," *People's Mass Book*, #106.

ACCLAMATION AT CONSECRATION:
  "Keep in Mind," *People's Mass Book*, #145.

ENDING ACCLAMATION:
  #190b, *People's Mass Book*.

THE SERVICE OF COMMUNION

THE "OUR FATHER"

RITE OF PEACE

FRACTION RITE:
  Litany of the "Lamb of God"

SONG:

> "Magnificat," *Hymnal for Young Christians,* Vol. II,
> Congregation Edition, p. 128.

PERIOD OF REFLECTION:
> Intermission

THE DISMISSAL RITE

PRAYER OF BENEDICTION:
> "We thank you, God, our grace," *Your Word Is Near,* p. 34.

BLESSING AND DISMISSAL

ANNOUNCEMENTS

RECESSIONAL

EIGHTEENTH SUNDAY AFTER PENTECOST II

Theme: Prayer: Fruit-Bearing

THE ENTRANCE RITE

INVITATION TO WORSHIP:
"Prayer comes from a deep sense of our incompleteness . . ."
through "This openness is the spirit of prayer," from "On
Prayer" by Thomas Merton at Darjeeling.

PROCESSIONAL:
"Longing for God," *Biblical Hymns and Psalms*, p. 100.

GREETING:
To you who come in peace to call God's name,
    I wish the Lord be with you.

PRAYER OF INVOCATION:
"O God, your name," *Your Word Is Near*, p. 45.

THE SERVICE OF THE WORD

FIRST READING:
Isaiah 5:1–7.

RESPONSE:
Psalm 80:8–19.

SECOND READING:
Philippians 4:6–9.

GOSPEL ACCLAMATION:
Any appropriate "Alleluia" known by congregation.

THE GOSPEL:
John 15:1–8.

GOSPEL ACCLAMATION:
Repeat from above.

HOMILY

GENERAL INTENTIONS

PERIOD OF REFLECTION:
Intermission

PROCESSIONAL

THE TABLE PRAYER

PREFACE:
"Table Prayer of the New Creation," *Discovery in Celebration,* p. 122.

HYMN OF PRAISE:
"Praise God from Whom All Blessings Flow," *People's Mass Book,* #46.

ACCLAMATION AT CONSECRATION

ENDING ACCLAMATION

THE SERVICE OF COMMUNION

THE "OUR FATHER"

RITE OF PEACE

FRACTION RITE:
Litany of the "Lamb of God"

SONG:
"Behold Among Men," *Biblical Hymns and Psalms,* p. 36.

PERIOD OF REFLECTION:
Intermission

THE DISMISSAL RITE

PRAYER OF BENEDICTION:
"Lord God, you sent your Son into the world," *Your Word Is Near*, p. 59.

BLESSING AND DISMISSAL

ANNOUNCEMENTS

RECESSIONAL:
"Strengthen for Service, Lord, These Hands," *The Hymnal of the Protestant Episcopal Church in the United States of America*, #201.

NINETEENTH SUNDAY AFTER PENTECOST II

Theme: God's Word Does Not Return to Him Void

THE ENTRANCE RITE

INVITATION TO WORSHIP:

The great King Solomon said: "Heaven cannot contain thee; how much less this house that I have built!" And yet the king of glory passed through the gates of a temple where Israel's pilgrims sought his face. The psalm we use this morning to begin our liturgy shares the astonishment of Solomon: "Will God indeed dwell with man on earth?" For us that wonder is surpassed. We have seen the Son of God pass through the gate of our nature and heard him speak of "the temple of his body." And this is not all. Assumed into that body our own selves become temples too—but we must throw open the gates of a generous heart: "If any man loves me, my Father will love him and we will come to him." We think of this as we sing: "Let him enter, the king of glory." Come, Lord Jesus!

PROCESSIONAL:

"The Lord's Is The Earth," *Twenty-Four Psalms and a Canticle*, p. 12.

GREETING:

May the God whose strength we seek
    be the source of our courage as we turn to him
    in his Son, Christ the Lord victorious.

PRAYER OF INVOCATION:

Recalling our need for continued healing, our continued need for remembering the body of Christ, we pray:
Lord God, our Father, you spoke of humanness
    and your Son became that Word.
You spoke of unity and harmony in your kingdom,
    and your Son was made flesh.
He lives among us,

healing the grateful and the ungrateful,
but only those with faith in him
are healed forever.
We come to give you thanks,
just as you have made us,
seeking you through your Word made flesh for us,
Jesus, in whose name we pray, now and forever.

THE SERVICE OF THE WORD

FIRST READING:
2 Kings 5:14–16.

RESPONSE:
"Cry Out With Joy to the Lord," *Twenty-Four Psalms and a Canticle*, p. 32.

SECOND READING:
2 Timothy 2:8–13.

GOSPEL ACCLAMATION:
"Alleluia! Alleluia!," *Biblical Hymns and Psalms*, p. 86.

THE GOSPEL:
Luke 17:11–19.

GOSPEL ACCLAMATION:
Repeat from above.

HOMILY

PROFESSION OF FAITH:
"Confession of Faith," *Discovery in Prayer*, p. 115.

GENERAL INTENTIONS

PERIOD OF REFLECTION:
Intermission

PROCESSIONAL

THE TABLE PRAYER

PREFACE:
"Eucharistic Prayer of Human Unity," *The Experimental Liturgy Book*, p. 100.

HYMN OF PRAISE:
"Praise the Lord of Heaven," *People's Mass Book*, #180.

ACCLAMATION AT CONSECRATION:
#235a, *People's Mass Book*.

ENDING ACCLAMATION

THE SERVICE OF COMMUNION

THE "OUR FATHER"

RITE OF PEACE

FRACTION RITE:
Litany of the "Lamb of God"

SONG:
"My Shepherd Is the Lord," *Twenty-Four Psalms and a Canticle*, p. 10.

PERIOD OF REFLECTION:
Intermission

THE DISMISSAL RITE

PRAYER OF BENEDICTION:
"How many times, God?" *Your Word Is Near*, p. 19.

BLESSING AND DISMISSAL

ANNOUNCEMENTS

RECESSIONAL:
   "Praise the Lord, O Heavens," *People's Mass Book.* #181.

TWENTIETH SUNDAY AFTER PENTECOST II

Theme: Perseverance in Prayer: Barometer of Faith

THE ENTRANCE RITE

INVITATION TO WORSHIP:
James 1:5-8. Erich Fromm in *Horizons of Hope*, p. 247, may
also be used.

PROCESSIONAL:
"Glorify the Lord with Me," *Biblical Hymns and Psalms*, p. 78.

GREETING:
To you who come in faith and in search
of the grace of God's love,
I wish peace and courage.
May the victorious Spirit of the risen Lord be with you.

PRAYER OF INVOCATION:
Recalling that those who ask anything of the Father in the
name of his Son will be heard, we gather in his name to
pray:
Eternal Father of all creation,
the prayer and the life of your Son
are inseparable and consistent.
His faithfulness is without end.
Today in this action around your Word
and at this table we seek him—
to make our own prayer and our own lives
one and the same.
To do this we need the same strength and perseverance
which you gave to him.
Do not forget us whom you have made
as we praise you in the name of your Son,
today and in all the days to come,
forever and ever.

THE SERVICE OF THE WORD

FIRST READING:
   Exodus 17:8–13.

RESPONSE:
   "My Help Comes from God," *Twenty-Four Psalms and a Canticle*, p. 40.

SECOND READING:
   2 Timothy 3:14–4:2.

GOSPEL ACCLAMATION:
   "Alleluia! Alleluia!," *Biblical Hymns and Psalms*, p. 86.

THE GOSPEL:
   Luke 18:1–8.

GOSPEL ACCLAMATION:
   Repeat from above.

HOMILY

GENERAL INTENTIONS

PERIOD OF REFLECTION:
   Intermission

PROCESSIONAL

THE TABLE PRAYER

PREFACE:
   #2, *Open Your Hearts*, p. 11.

HYMN OF PRAISE:
   "Holy, Holy, Holy," *People's Mass Book*, #106.

ACCLAMATION AT CONSECRATION:
   #190b, *People's Mass Book*.

ENDING ACCLAMATION:
"You Alone Are Holy," *Biblical Hymns and Psalms*, Vol. II,
p. 52.

THE SERVICE OF COMMUNION

THE "OUR FATHER"

RITE OF PEACE

FRACTION RITE:
Litany of the "Lamb of God"

SONG:
"Without Seeing You," *People's Mass Book*, #173.

PERIOD OF REFLECTION:
Intermission

THE DISMISSAL RITE

PRAYER OF BENEDICTION:
The road to your presence and your kingdom
   is long and winding,
      but with your loving presence ever calling,
      we do not give way to confusion and despair.
We realize through this sacramental sign,
   that we must hold one another's arms,
   and that with patience and kindness
      the longest of journeys can be swift and joy-filled—
      life can be a continuous adventure of discovering
      your presence behind each smile and each tear.
All glory and praise be to you our God,
   in the name of your Son Jesus
   in whose body we find our strength,
   and in whose Spirit we find our joy,
      forever and ever.

BLESSING AND DISMISSAL

ANNOUNCEMENTS

RECESSIONAL:
"All Men on Earth," *People's Mass Book*, #36.

TWENTY-FIRST SUNDAY AFTER PENTECOST II

Theme: Mission Sunday: To Bring Good News to the Poor

THE ENTRANCE RITE

INVITATION TO WORSHIP:

In today's liturgy we think back to the close of the Easter
season and Pentecost. We remember the words of Jesus:
"Go into the whole world and proclaim the good news to the
whole of creation." He prepared the apostles to know and
accept the Holy Spirit; they were not to be left abandoned
and helpless: "You shall receive power when the Holy Spirit
comes upon you, and you shall be witnesses for me in
Jerusalem and in Judea, and in Samaria, and even to the very
ends of the earth." Today we unite ourselves to the whole
Catholic community in the world as we pray over our mission
as God's people. It is in union with all those who have taken
seriously the mandate to carry the Good News to every corner
of the world that we sing in praise of our God.

PROCESSIONAL:

"Praise, My Soul, the King of Heaven," *People's Mass Book,*
#183.

GREETING:

The Spirit of the Lord is upon us,
    fully confirming us in the mission
    of preaching the Good News to every creature.

PRAYER OF INVOCATION:

With hearts grateful for the indwelling of the Spirit, let us
pray:
Father, we thank you for the gift of your Spirit
    who makes us mindful of our desires
    to search for truth and love.
May we always show to you fitting praise and thanks
    by each becoming a sign and cause of unity
    within the family of your people.

205

Let our day be a new Pentecost,
　　that we may accept the promise of your Son,
　　that you would give us a new heart,
　　and put a new spirit within us.
All glory be to you, Father, and to your Son,
　　and to your Holy Spirit, now and forever.
(Adapted from *Eucharistic Liturgies*, p. 82.)

THE SERVICE OF THE WORD

FIRST READING:
　　Ecclesiasticus 35:11b(15)–17(21).

RESPONSE:
　　Silent reflection.

SECOND READING:
　　1 Peter 5:5–9.

GOSPEL ACCLAMATION:
　　"Send Forth Your Light and Your Truth," *Twenty-Four Psalms and a Canticle*, p. 20.

THE GOSPEL:
　　Luke 4:16–21.

GOSPEL ACCLAMATION:
　　Repeat from above.

HOMILY

PROFESSION OF FAITH:
　　Mission Creed (see Second Sunday of Easter II, this volume).

GENERAL INTENTIONS

PERIOD OF REFLECTION:
　　Intermission

PROCESSIONAL

THE TABLE PRAYER

PREFACE:
"The Canon of the Pilgrim Church," *The Experimental Liturgy Book*, p. 73.

HYMN OF PRAISE:
"Holy, Holy, Holy! Lord God Almighty," *People's Mass Book*, #184.

ACCLAMATION AT CONSECRATION:
#235a, *People's Mass Book*.

ENDING ACCLAMATION

THE SERVICE OF COMMUNION

THE "OUR FATHER"

RITE OF PEACE

FRACTION RITE:
Litany of the "Lamb of God"

SONG:
None today. Reading excerpted from *He Is the Still Point of the Turning World*, pp. 16, 17, 18.

PERIOD OF REFLECTION:
Intermission

THE DISMISSAL RITE

PRAYER OF BENEDICTION:
We give you thanks
    that your wisdom never fails us,
    that your strength will never let us down.
We have taken the bread and wine

which give life, and heard your promise
to be with us always.
We are confident that your Word is true
and that you, our God, will help us and support us.
Stay with us, Father, throughout this day and every day;
make us to be ever more your people,
loyal and true to the promises we have made.
We ask this in the name of Jesus Christ,
our brother and our Lord,
who draws all things to himself
and gives them the promise of life.
All glory be to you, Father, and to your Son,
and to the Holy Spirit, now and forever.

BLESSING AND DISMISSAL

ANNOUNCEMENTS

RECESSIONAL:
"Now Thank We All Our God," *People's Mass Book,* #178.

TWENTY-SECOND SUNDAY AFTER PENTECOST II

Theme: The Goodness of Creation

THE ENTRANCE RITE

INVITATION TO WORSHIP:
Before we formally begin our liturgy today, let us listen to a
reading which delightfully describes with great fantasy one
author's concept of the great moment of creation. Behind its
humor and spirit of merriment lies the important truth that
all creation is a participation in the powerful, creative
relationship of the Trinity. The reading is from *The Third
Peacock*. (Read pp. 11–12, to "*per omnia saecula saeculorum.
Amen.*")
It is in the presence of this God that we are gathered together
this morning—right in the middle of this city where his people
live and die. It is in the tempo and spirit of this creativeness
that we get together to celebrate our relationship which, if
creative, makes us sharers in the mystery of the Trinity—
the mystery of the living, saving God: Father, Son, and Spirit.

PROCESSIONAL:
"All the Earth," *People's Mass Book*, #141.

GREETING:
To you who assemble in peace
    to find peace and courage,
    to share in the victory of the Word made flesh,
I wish blessings, and may the Spirit of the Lord be with you.

PRAYER OF INVOCATION:
Mindful of the needs we share, or our weakness as individuals,
and our strength as a community of faith, we pray:
God, our Father, we anticipate with great joy
    the fulfillment of your promises to us.
Your Son, your Word made flesh, your creative Word,
    forms us as your people.
Stand by us as you stood by your people in the desert,

as we seek to overcome those things
which divide and bring death—
so that we may share in the triumph of your Son
and give you all glory now and forever and ever.

THE SERVICE OF THE WORD

FIRST READING:
Wisdom 11:22(23)–12:1.

RESPONSE:
"Psalm 150," *People's Mass Book,* #163.

SECOND READING:
1 Thessalonians 4:1–3a, 9–10; 5:12–18.

RESPONSE:
Reflection on "Pied Beauty," *Gerard Manley Hopkins,* p. 30.

GOSPEL ACCLAMATION:
"Alleluia! Alleluia!," *People's Mass Book,* p. 86.

THE GOSPEL:
Luke 19:1–10.

GOSPEL ACCLAMATION:
Repeat from above.

HOMILY

GENERAL INTENTIONS

PERIOD OF REFLECTION:
Intermission

PROCESSIONAL

THE TABLE PRAYER

PREFACE:
Indeed it is right and just to give you thanks, Father;

it is our privilege and our salvation.
You have called us to serve you as Christians,
    and this we do gladly.
We stand before you today
    to thank you for all your gifts.
All that is, is yours,
    and you have given all to us.
We thank you for the beauties of nature,
    for the wonders of human invention,
    for the companionship of friends,
    for the gifts of your loving Spirit.
In gratitude we have gathered together today
    to remind each other
    of what we are and what we have.
May we never stop growing
    in love of you and one another.
We come together in the name of Jesus your Son;
    it is the spirit of his presence
    that makes us burst into song
    as we sing together:

HYMN OF PRAISE:
    "Praise to the Lord," *People's Mass Book*, #175.

ACCLAMATION AT CONSECRATION:
    #235a, *People's Mass Book*.

ENDING ACCLAMATION:
    "Praise to the Lord" (cited above), third verse.

THE SERVICE OF COMMUNION

THE "OUR FATHER"

RITE OF PEACE

FRACTION RITE:
    Litany of the "Lamb of God"

SONG:
    "Priestly People," *People's Mass Book*, #146.

PERIOD OF REFLECTION:
  Intermission

THE DISMISSAL RITE

PRAYER OF BENEDICTION:
  "We are the work of your hands, O God," *Your Word Is Near*, p. 21.

BLESSING AND DISMISSAL

ANNOUNCEMENTS

RECESSIONAL:
  "Praise the Lord, O Heavens," *People's Mass Book*, #181.

TWENTY-THIRD SUNDAY AFTER PENTECOST II

Theme: A Harvest Festival

THE ENTRANCE RITE

INVITATION TO WORSHIP:

We have, in recent days, celebrated part of this autumn
harvest time by reflecting on the holiness of God's people,
living and dead. Today we give a bit more attention to
ourselves and the harvest of our own service. With some
mixed feelings, perhaps, it is time to begin to look at our
own harvest if it is true that we are to be known by our
fruits; for it is harvest time. Relaxed afternoon shadows are
long now, and lean. The sweat and toil of many years is
beginning to slow down some of our community, and we
gather about these faithful ones today to celebrate with them
the benefits of their years.
Continue with "The promise spring made long ago" in *Listen
to Love*, p. 266. Then the people join the reader in praying
Joel 2:24–26.

PROCESSIONAL:

"My Soul Is Longing," *People's Mass Book*, #161.

GREETING:

Peace and blessings to you from our Lord Jesus Christ,
    who has revealed to us
    the love of God our Father for us
    who are called to be his sons and daughters.

PRAYER OF INVOCATION:

Mindful of the Father's loving concern for us, let us pray:
Our Father, God of our lives,
    we give you thanks for your gift of time,
    for the blessing of each moment in which
    the kingdom of heaven sinks its roots within us.
Our years, Father, have been full—
    rich with the harvest of life in togetherness,

213

heavy with the fatigue and rewards of our work,
graced with the pains of birth and growth.
But above all, Father, they are completed years.
We can have no regrets
    but can only say at this moment of pause
    that we would not have had them otherwise.
Time has made us what we are—
    your children—
    and we offer you our thanks.
In peace, let us hear the Word of God.

THE SERVICE OF THE WORD

FIRST READING:
    1 Kings 17:2–16.

RESPONSE:
    Ephesians 3:14–19. Change "his" to "your"; "you" and "your"
    to "we, us, our."

THE GOSPEL:
    Mark 12:41–44.
    This liturgy was originally used as a setting for the anointing
    of elderly members of the congregation; the rite of anointing
    is administered at this time.

THE TABLE PRAYER

PREFACE:
    It is fitting for us to praise you,
        life-giving and merciful Father,
        especially at this season
        when all life seems to turn inward
        to gather strength for the new burst of life
        that will come in springtime.
    In gratitude for the favors received
        by the gift of the sacrament of anointing,
        and the fullness of your life in creation,

we open our hearts
to all the joys, hopes, sorrows, and anxieties
of the people of our time
in order that, united in Christ,
all may reach the kingdom prepared for us.
In this spirit of oneness, we join with all creation
and burst into one great song of praise:

HYMN OF PRAISE:
"Praise, My Soul, the King of Heaven," *People's Mass Book,*
#184.

ACCLAMATION AT CONSECRATION:
#190b, *People's Mass Book.*

ENDING ACCLAMATION:
"Praise God From Whom All Blessings Flow," *People's Mass
Book,* #45.

THE SERVICE OF COMMUNION

THE "OUR FATHER"

RITE OF PEACE

FRACTION RITE:
Litany of the "Lamb of God"

SONG:
"My Shepherd Is the Lord," *Twenty-Four Psalms and a
Canticle,* p. 10.

PERIOD OF REFLECTION:
Intermission

THE DISMISSAL RITE

PRAYER OF BENEDICTION

BLESSING AND DISMISSAL:
Ephesians 1:17–23.

ANNOUNCEMENTS

RECESSIONAL:
"Now Thank We All Our God," *People's Mass Book,* #178.

TWENTY-FOURTH SUNDAY AFTER PENTECOST II

Theme: The Harvest: Suffering Because We Are Prophets

THE ENTRANCE RITE

INVITATION TO WORSHIP:
Today, gathered as God's people, we consider the harvest of
shame—the harvest of suffering that can be expected by
those who realize their prophetic role as members of the body
of Christ. As the prophets before us have been treated, so
can we expect to be treated by those of little faith. We
remember the condition of Job. In part of the narrative, Satan
has challenged Job's faith and the quality of God's creation.
To meet the challenge . . . (*here continue with Job 2:6–10*).

PROCESSIONAL:
"We Gather Together," *People's Mass Book*, #53.

GREETING:
Blessed be God, the Father of all consolation,
    who comforts us in all our suffering,
    so that we may in turn comfort others in theirs.

PRAYER OF INVOCATION:
"Father, you have given your Son to us," *Your Word Is Near*,
p. 58.

THE SERVICE OF THE WORD

FIRST READING:
Amos 7:12–15.

SECOND READING:
"Song of the Suffering Servant": Isaiah 50:4–9.

RESPONSE:
Matthew 10:17–20, 26–27.

GOSPEL ACCLAMATION:
"Alleluia! Alleluia!," *Biblical Hymns and Psalms*, p. 86.

THE GOSPEL:
Mark 6:1–6.

GOSPEL ACCLAMATION:
Repeat from above.

HOMILY

GENERAL INTENTIONS

PERIOD OF REFLECTION:
Intermission

PROCESSIONAL

THE TABLE PRAYER

PREFACE:
See Seventeenth Sunday after Pentecost I.

HYMN OF PRAISE

ACCLAMATION AT CONSECRATION:
#235a, *People's Mass Book.*

ENDING ACCLAMATION:
"You Alone Are Holy," *Biblical Hymns and Psalms*, Vol. II,
p. 52.

THE SERVICE OF COMMUNION

THE "OUR FATHER"

RITE OF PEACE

FRACTION RITE:
Litany of the "Lamb of God"

SONG:
"Priestly People," *People's Mass Book*, #146.

PERIOD OF REFLECTION:
Intermission

THE DISMISSAL RITE

PRAYER OF BENEDICTION:
"We have your promise, God," *Your Word Is Near*, p. 62.
Add to the third sentence ". . . looking beyond our own hurt
to the understanding and comfort we can bring others in
their distress."

BLESSING AND DISMISSAL

ANNOUNCEMENTS

RECESSIONAL:
"Glorify the Lord With Me," *People's Mass Book*, #164.

FESTIVAL OF THE ASSUMPTION II

This liturgy is the same as the Festival of the Assumption I with the exceptions that follow:

FIRST READING:
Revelation: 11:19; 12:1-6, 10a.

SECOND READING:
Luke 1:39-45.

FEAST OF ALL SAINTS II

Theme: The Unity of the Faithful

THE ENTRANCE RITE

INVITATION TO WORSHIP:
This liturgy, above all other celebrations of the Lord's supper,
directs our attention to the unity of faithful people who
search so restlessly for their God and who, because of their
determination in faith, finally are victorious. Their prize is
peace with the Father forever. We anticipate our own victory
and are glad for the success of those who have gone before
us. In a dream recorded by St. John in his Book of
Revelation we get in fantasy a glimpse of that victory
celebration. *(Here read Revelation 7:9–17.)*

PROCESSIONAL:
"All You Nations," *People's Mass Book,* #142.

GREETING:
May courage and strength be yours,
  you who seek peace,
  and may the Spirit of the Lord be with you
  until you finally share in glory.

PRAYER OF INVOCATION:
Remembering that in this situation, gathered as we are, there
is the power and the strength of the Lord's presence, let us
pray:
Father, we praise you
  for what you have accomplished in your Son Jesus.
For after all these many years,
  after all that men have done to confuse his image,
  he remains.
Your invitation and your kingdom
  are still possible for us and still at hand
  for those who can say "yes" and who choose
  to be counted among those he called "blessed."

221

It is in his name
   that we are gathered to give you praise,
   now and forever and ever.

THE SERVICE OF THE WORD

FIRST READING:
   Entry for January 16, 1923, *Journal of a Soul*, p. 106.

RESPONSE:
   See adaptation from 1 Corinthians 4:11 in Feast of All Saints
   I (Vol. I).

GOSPEL ACCLAMATION:
   "Alleluia, Alleluia, Alleluia," *People's Mass Book*, #86c.

THE GOSPEL:
   Matthew 5:1–12.

GOSPEL ACCLAMATION:
   Repeat from above.

HOMILY

GENERAL INTENTIONS

PERIOD OF REFLECTION:
   Intermission

PROCESSIONAL

THE TABLE PRAYER

PREFACE:
   See Preface in Feast of All Saints I (Vol. I).

HYMN OF PRAISE

ACCLAMATION AT CONSECRATION

ENDING ACCLAMATION

THE SERVICE OF COMMUNION

THE "OUR FATHER"

RITE OF PEACE

FRACTION RITE:
Litany of the "Lamb of God"

SONG:
"Keep in Mind," *People's Mass Book,* #145.

PERIOD OF REFLECTION:
Intermission

THE DISMISSAL RITE

PRAYER OF BENEDICTION:
See Prayer of Benediction, Feast of All Saints I (Vol. I).

BLESSING AND DISMISSAL

ANNOUNCEMENTS

RECESSIONAL:
"For All the Saints," *The Hymnal of the Protestant Episcopal Church in the United States of America,* #126.

FESTIVAL OF ALL SOULS II

Theme: Grains of Wheat Falling on the Ground

THE ENTRANCE RITE
The minister enters in silence.

GREETING:
> Come and let us worship the Lord,
>> for he is our God,
>> and we are his people.

PRAYER OF INVOCATION:
> *(Read by all)*
> Father, merciful God,
>> we come to adore you, the king of life.
> Through your Son, Jesus Christ,
>> the hope of a blessed resurrection has dawned forever.
> For to those who have faith in you
>> life does not cease; it merely changes.
> Keeping our eyes fixed on the surrender of Jesus to you,
>> we proclaim that death is not the end
>> and that you are a God of the living,
>> with whom all things are safe.

THE SERVICE OF THE WORD

FIRST READING:
> First paragraph, Reading II, Common of Dead, *American Interim Breviary,* p. 1427.

RESPONSE:
> "Autumn Prayer," *Listen to Love,* p. 271.

THE GOSPEL:
> John 12:23–26a.

HOMILY

GENERAL INTENTIONS

PERIOD OF REFLECTION:
Intermission

THE TABLE PRAYER

PREFACE:
See Second Sunday of Easter II, this volume.

HYMN OF PRAISE:
"Holy, Holy, Holy! Lord God Almighty," *People's Mass Book*,
#184.

ACCLAMATION AT CONSECRATION:
#190b, *People's Mass Book*.

ENDING ACCLAMATION:
"You Alone Are Holy," *Biblical Hymns and Psalms*, Vol. II,
p. 52.

THE SERVICE OF COMMUNION

THE "OUR FATHER"

RITE OF PEACE

FRACTION RITE:
Litany of the "Lamb of God"

SONG:
"Yes, I Shall Arise," *People's Mass Book*, #174.

PERIOD OF REFLECTION:
Intermission

THE DISMISSAL RITE

PRAYER OF BENEDICTION:
You are rightly to be praised, Father,

and with reason is your name blessed today and all days.
For you have called us out of darkness
   into the light of your world
   and given us promise of endless summer
   and new life in your kingdom.
In Jesus' name we pray now and forever and ever.

BLESSING AND DISMISSAL

ANNOUNCEMENTS

RECESSIONAL:
   "Alleluia! The Strife Is O'er," *People's Mass Book*, #34.

FEAST OF CHRIST KING II

The same as liturgy for this feast in year I with exception of
Second Reading. The following may be used: Colossians 1:12–20.

FEAST OF THANKSGIVING II

Theme: Reaping the Harvest Together

THE ENTRANCE RITE

INVITATION TO WORSHIP:
This is a liturgy about the earth as our home, a liturgy
which concludes our month-long reflection upon the harvest
time, and one which tries to help us build a proper sense of
thankfulness. Too often the theme of a Thanksgiving liturgy
comes dangerously close to the prayer of the Pharisee: "Lord,
I give you thanks that I am not as the rest of men." They
are hungry; I am fed. They steal; I protect my belongings
and work for what I have. With this in mind, we begin to
look more deeply into this festival day to search for the
blessings that a Christian must value most—those that go
beyond the material.

PROCESSIONAL:
"Seek the Face of the Lord," *Twenty-Four Psalms and a
Canticle*, p. 13.

GREETING:
Blessings and peace to you from God our Father
to whom we give thanks
in union with all of creation.

PRAYER OF INVOCATION:
"Autumn Prayer," *Listen to Love*, p. 271.

THE SERVICE OF THE WORD

FIRST READING:
From *History of the Pilgrim Colony*, in *The Experimental
Liturgy Book*, p. 174.

RESPONSE:
"The Canticle of the Sun," *The Peace of St. Francis*, p. 241.

228

SECOND READING:
Romans 12:6–8.

GOSPEL ACCLAMATION:
"Alleluia! Alleluia!," *Biblical Hymns and Psalms*, p. 86.

THE GOSPEL:
John 15:1–8.

GOSPEL ACCLAMATION:
Repeat from above.

HOMILY

GENERAL INTENTIONS

PERIOD OF REFLECTION:
Intermission

PROCESSIONAL

THE TABLE PRAYER

PREFACE:
"Canon for a Day of Thanksgiving," *Eucharistic Liturgies*,
p. 199.

HYMN OF PRAISE:
"Crown Him With Many Crowns," *People's Mass Book*, #49.

ACCLAMATION AT CONSECRATION:
#235a, *People's Mass Book*.

ENDING ACCLAMATION:
"You Alone Are Holy," *Biblical Hymns and Psalms*, Vol. II,
p. 52.

THE SERVICE OF COMMUNION

THE "OUR FATHER"

RITE OF PEACE

FRACTION RITE:
Litany of the "Lamb of God"

SONG:
"Shepherd of Souls," *People's Mass Book*, #123.

PERIOD OF REFLECTION:
Intermission

THE DISMISSAL RITE

PRAYER OF BENEDICTION:
"Father, despite our best," *Home Celebrations*, p. 87.

BLESSING AND DISMISSAL

ANNOUNCEMENTS

RECESSIONAL:
"Now Thank We All Our God," *People's Mass Book*, #178.

SELECTED SOURCES

PREFACES AND EUCHARISTIC PRAYERS

Discovery in Celebration, ed. Robert J. Heyer, Jack Podsiadlo, and Richard Payne (New York: Paulist Press, Copyright 1970 by The Missionary Society of St. Paul the Apostle in the State of New York).

The English-Latin Sacramentary for the United States of America, Catholic Book Publishing Co., New York, Copyright 1966 by Bishops' Commission on the Liturgical Apostolate; English translation of orations, prefaces, and similar material, Copyright 1957, 1961, 1966 by P. J. Kenedy & Sons.

Eucharistic Liturgies, ed. John Gallen, S.J. (New York: Newman Press, Copyright 1969 by The Missionary Society of St. Paul the Apostle in the State of New York).

The Experimental Liturgy Book, ed. Robert F. Hoey (New York: Herder and Herder, 1969).

Open Your Hearts, Huub Oosterhuis (New York: Herder and Herder, 1971).

The Underground Mass Book, ed. Stephen J. McNierney (Baltimore: Helicon, Copyright 1968 by Stephen J. McNierney).

STATEMENTS OF BELIEF

The Experimental Liturgy Book, ed. Robert F. Hoey (New York: Herder and Herder, 1969).

The Underground Mass Book, ed. Stephen J. McNierney (Baltimore: Helicon, Copyright 1968 by Stephen J. McNierney).

PRAYERS (INVOCATION, OFFERTORY, BENEDICTION)

Eucharistic Liturgies, ed. John Gallen, S.J. (New York: Newman Press, Copyright 1969 by The Missionary Society of St. Paul the Apostle in the State of New York).

Interrobang, Norman C. Habel (Philadelphia: Fortress Press, 1969).

231

Your Word Is Near, Huub Oosterhuis (New York: Newman Press, Copyright 1968 by The Missionary Society of St. Paul the Apostle in the State of New York).

GENERAL INTENTIONS

Your Word Is Near, Huub Oosterhuis (New York: Newman Press, Copyright 1968 by The Missionary Society of St. Paul the Apostle in the State of New York).

WEDDINGS, BAPTISMS, SPECIAL OCCASIONS

Home Celebrations, Lawrence E. Moser (New York: Newman Press, Copyright 1970 by The Missionary Society of St. Paul the Apostle in the State of New York).
Manual of Celebration, Robert Hovda (Washington, D.C.: The Liturgical Conference, Copyright 1969 by the International Committee on English in the Liturgy, Inc.).

READINGS, RESPONSES, INVITATIONS TO WORSHIP

The Jerusalem Bible, ed. Alexander Jones (New York: Doubleday & Co., Inc., 1966).
Lectionary for Mass (English Translation Approved by the National Conference of Catholic Bishops and Confirmed by the Apostolic See), *The Roman Missal* (Revised by Decree of the Second Vatican Council and Published by Authority of Pope Paul VI) (New York: Catholic Book Publishing Co., Copyright 1970 by the Confraternity of Christian Doctrine; International Copyright under International Copyright Union; all rights reserved under Pan-American Copyright Convention/English translation of the Introduction, Titles, Summaries and Antiphons Copyright 1969, International Committee on English in the Liturgy, Inc. All rights reserved).
Belief in Human Life, Anthony T. Padovano (New York: Paulist Press, Copyright 1969 by The Missionary Society of St. Paul the Apostle in the State of New York).

Children's Liturgies, ed. Virginia Sloyan and Gabe Huck (Washington, D.C.: The Liturgical Conference, 1970).

The Constitution on the Church, ed. Edward H. Peters (Glen Rock, N.J.: Deus Books, Paulist Press, Copyright 1965 by The Missionary Society of St. Paul the Apostle in the State of New York).

The Cost of Discipleship, Dietrich Bonhoeffer (New York: The Macmillan Co., 1963).

Discovery in Prayer, ed. Robert Heyer and Richard Payne (New York: Paulist Press, Copyright 1969 by The Missionary Society of St. Paul the Apostle in the State of New York).

Discovery in Song, ed. Robert Heyer (New York: Paulist Press, Copyright 1970 by The Missionary Society of St. Paul the Apostle in the State of New York).

Discovery in Word, ed. Robert J. Heyer (New York: Paulist Press, Copyright 1968 by The Missionary Society of St. Paul the Apostle in the State of New York).

The Documents of Vatican II, ed. Walter Abbott (New York: The America Press, 1966).

The Fables of Aesop, retold by Joseph Jacobs, reprinted by permission of The Macmillan Co. in *Coping,* Macmillan Gateway English Program, ed. Marjorie B. Smiley, *et al.* (New York: The Macmillan Co., 1966).

Faces of Freedom, ed. Adrianne Blue and Louis Savary (Winona, Minn.: St. Mary's College Press, 1969).

Free to Live, Free to Die, Malcolm Boyd (New York: Holt, Rinehart and Winston, Copyright 1967 by Malcolm Boyd).

God Speaks, Charles Peguy (New York: Pantheon Books, Inc., 1945).

He Is the Still Point of the Turning World, Mark Link, (Chicago: Argus Communications, 1971).

I've Got a Name, Holt's Impact Series, ed. Charlotte Brooks and Lawana Trout (New York: Holt, Rinehart & Winston, Inc., 1968).

Horizons of Hope, ed. Adrianne Blue and Louis Savary (Winona, Minn.: St. Mary's College Press, 1969).

Hymn of the Universe, Teilhard de Chardin, (New York: Harper & Row, Inc., 1965).

Journal of a Soul, Pope John XXIII (New York: McGraw-Hill Book Co., Copyright 1965 by Geoffrey Chapman, Ltd.).

Listen to Love, ed. Louis M. Savary (New York: Regina Press, 1969).

The Little Prince, Antoine de Saint-Exupery (New York: Harcourt, Brace & World, 1943).

The Living Shakespeare, ed. O. J. Campbell (New York: The Macmillan Co., 1949).

My Life with Martin Luther King, Jr., Coretta Scott King (New York: Holt, Rinehart & Winston, 1969).

The New St. Andrew Bible Missal (New York: Benziger Brothers, Copyright 1966 by the Abbaye de St. Andre, Bruges, Belgium).

A New Catechism (New York: Herder and Herder, 1967).

95 Poems, e. e. cummings (New York: Harcourt, Brace & World, 1958).

Prayers, Michel Quoist (New York: Sheed & Ward, 1963).

Prayers for Pagans, Roger Bush (Dayton: Pflaum Press, 1969).

Prayers, Poems & Songs, Huub Oosterhuis (New York: Herder and Herder, 1970).

The Prophet, Kahlil Gibran (New York: Alfred A. Knopf, Renewal Copyright 1951 by Administrators C. T. A. of Kahlil Gibran Estate, & Mary G. Gibran).

Ritual and Life, ed. Maureen P. Collins, *et al.* (Winona, Minn.: St. Mary's College Press, 1970).

The Secular City, Harvey Cox (New York: The Macmillan Co., 1965).

Shaping of a Self, ed. Louis M. Savary, Jane C. Carter, and Charles Burke (Winona, Minn.: St. Mary's College Press, 1970).

The Sins of the Just, John H. McGoey (Milwaukee: Bruce Publishing Co., 1963).

Tender of Wishes, James Carroll (New York: Newman Press, Copyright 1969 by The Missionary Society of St. Paul the Apostle in the State of New York).

The Third Peacock, Robert Farrar Capon (Garden City, N.Y.: Doubleday & Co., 1971).

To Be Alive!, Alastair Reid (New York: The Macmillan Co., 1966).

To Kill a Mockingbird, Harper Lee (New York: J. P. Lippincott Co., Copyright 1960 by Harper Lee).

That Man Is You, Louis Evely (New York: Newman Press, Copyright 1964 by The Missionary Society of St. Paul the Apostle in the State of New York).

A *Tree Grows In Brooklyn,* Betty Smith (New York: Harper & Row
   Publishers, Inc., Copyright 1947 by Betty Smith).
The Underground Mass Book, ed. Stephen W. McNierney (Balti-
   more: Helicon, Copyright 1968 by Stephen W. McNierney).
The Unexpected Universe, Loren Eiseley (New York: Harcourt,
   Brace & World, Copyright 1969 by Loren Eiseley).
The Velveteen Rabbit, Margery Williams (Garden City, N.Y.:
   Doubleday, 1922).
Whitman, ed. Leslie A. Fiedler (New York: Dell Publishing Co.,
   Inc., Copyright 1959 by Richard Wilbur).

MAGAZINES:

Critic
The Christian Herald
Ladies Home Journal
Life
Look
Sign
Voices: The Art and Science of Psychotherapy

MUSIC

Biblical Hymns and Psalms (Cincinnati: World Library of Sacred
   Music, 1965).
Biblical Hymns and Psalms, Vol. II (Cincinnati: World Library of
   Sacred Music, 1970).
Come Alive, Ray Repp (Chicago: F. E. L. Church Publications,
   Ltd., 1967).
*The Hymnal of the Protestant Episcopal Church in the United
   States of America* (New York: The Church Pension Fund,
   1940).
Hymnal for Young Christians (Chicago: F. E. L. Church Publica-
   tions, Ltd. 1967), Complete edition.
Hymnal for Young Christians, Vol. II (Chicago: F. E. L. Church
   Publications, Ltd. 1969).
Hymns for Now I (St. Louis: Walther League, 1967).

Our Parish Prays and Sings (Collegeville, Minn.: The Liturgical Press, Copyright 1959 by the Order of St. Benedict, Inc.).

People's Mass Book (Cincinnati: World Library of Sacred Music, 1970).

Psalms for Singing, Book One, S. Somerville (Cincinnati: World Library of Sacred Music, 1960).

Thirty Songs and Two Canticles (Toledo: Gregorian Institute of America, Copyright 1957 by The Grail, England).

Twenty-Four Psalms and a Canticle, Joseph Gelineau (Toledo: Gregorian Institute of America, Copyright 1955 by The Grail, England).

Yes, The Spirit Is A-Movin', Carey Landry (Washington, D.C.: Theological College Publications, 1969).

Hand in Hand, Joseph Wise (Cincinnati: World Library of Sacred Music, 1968).

INDEX OF THEMES, FESTIVALS, AND SPECIAL OCCASIONS